133431

635.944
Jam        James, Theodore

Flowering bulbs
indoors and out

DUE DATE

|  |  |  |  |
|---|---|---|---|
|  |  |  |  |
|  |  |  |  |
|  |  |  |  |
|  |  |  |  |
|  |  |  |  |
|  |  |  |  |
|  |  |  |  |
|  |  |  |  |
|  |  |  |  |
|  |  |  |  |
|  |  |  |  |

# FLOWERING BULBS

# INDOORS

# AND OUT

# FLOWERING BULBS
# INDOORS
# AND OUT

*Theodore James, Jr.*

*Photographs by Harry Haralambou*

*Macmillan Publishing Company*
NEW YORK

*Maxwell Macmillan Canada*
TORONTO

*Maxwell Macmillan International*
NEW YORK  OXFORD  SINGAPORE  SYDNEY

*The author and photographer*
*dedicate this book to*
*two very special people:*
*Stella Zinon and L. Herndon Werth*

Macmillan Publishing Company
866 Third Avenue, New York, NY 10022

Maxwell Macmillan Canada, Inc.
1200 Eglinton Avenue East, Suite 200
Don Mills, Ontario M3C 3N1

Macmillan Publishing Company is part of the Maxwell
Communication Group of Companies.

Library of Congress Cataloging-in-Publication Data

James, Theodore.
    Flowering bulbs indoors and out/Theodore James, Jr.;
photographs by Harry Haralambou.
      p.  cm.
    Includes index.
    ISBN 0-02-558915-6
    1. Bulbs.  I. Title.
SB425.J36   1991
635.9'44—dc20                 90-26016
                                CIP

Macmillan books are available at special discounts for bulk
purchases for sales promotions, premiums, fund-raising, or
educational use. For details, contact:

Special Sales Director
Macmillan Publishing Company
866 Third Avenue
New York, NY 10022

10  9  8  7  6  5  4  3  2  1

*Printed in the United States of America*

# Contents

# *Acknowledgments*

We are grateful for the kind cooperation of the following: Hotel des Indes, The Hague, Holland; Restaurant de Bokkedoorns, Zeeweg, Holland; KLM; Netherlands Flower Bulb Institute; Willem Schouten of the Netherlands Board of Tourism; Mrs. Sally Munnig-Schmidt, Baron de Vos van Steenwyk, Baroness Van Heccheren van Brandtenburg, Baron van Zuylen van Nyeveld de Haar, Willem Hoeben, Carla Oldenburger-Ebbert, Renny Blaisse, Madame Mien Ruys, Sernande Hora Siccama, and Count and Countess van Limburg Stirum, all of the Netherlands, and all of whom shared their beautiful gardens with us; the Virginia Board of Tourism; the Belgian Government Tourist Bureau; Robert Dash; Margie Kerr; Robert La Rue Associates; Mrs. Alice Levian for sharing her loverly garden with us; Pat and Bill Milford; Lucille Siracusano of Feather Hill Country Flowers and Gifts, Southold, New York; Alfred and Delfina Smith; Thomas and Martina Rheinhardt, Creative Landscaping, East Hampton, New York; The Garden Club of Virginia; Metro Richmond Convention and Visitors Bureau, Richmond, Virginia; Marietta Silvestre; Mrs. Carleton Cole, our agent; our editor, Pam Hoenig; and our editor's assistant, Justin Schwartz.

# *Introduction*

What would any garden, anywhere, be without the glorious bloom of bulbs? Certainly, no spring garden even begins to be complete without the resplendent display of crocuses, tulips, hyacinths, and daffodils. Once planted, most of these bulbs bloom year in and year out, with minimal and often no care whatsoever.

In the summer, the stately lilies, riotous dahlias, shade-loving tuberous begonias and caladiums, highly scented acidanthera and tuberose, and others all add touches of class to the annual or perennial garden. Fall brings only a handful of blooming bulbs, but the charm of autumn crocus and colchicum naturalized in a woodland setting cannot be overlooked.

And finally, in the winter, bulbs such as amaryllis and forced tulips and daffodils continue to cheer us from their perches on windowsills and throughout the house.

Most bulbs are very inexpensive, easy to plant, and grow and reward us with lavish bloom and gratification year after year. But you must make sure the bulbs you plant will grow in your area. So, before you sit down to plan your garden, check the United States Department of Agriculture map on page 8 and find out which zone you live in. As you browse through the bulb entries, note only those bulbs appropriate to your particular zone. Once you've eliminated those not suitable, you are ready to make your selection.

Even if you're a beginning gardener, if you follow the instructions that follow, you should have undreamed-of success with our bulb plantings. Happy gardening!

*Chapter One*

# A SHORT HISTORY OF FLOWERING BULBS

The commercial history of flowering bulbs goes back to the ancient Minoan civilization that thrived on the island of Crete around four thousand years ago. For them, the crocus was the bulb of choice.

It is the tulip, however, that has the most colorful history of the bulbs. Prior to 1554, tulips had never been seen in Europe. That year, Austrian emperor Ferdinand I sent Ogier Ghiselin de Busbecque from Flanders, which at the time was subject to Austria, to Constantinople in Turkey to negotiate peace with Sultan Suleiman the Magnificent, who had invaded Hungary and laid siege to Vienna. De Busbecque was successful in his diplomacy, but more to the point, his keen interest in botany led to the introduction of the tulip in Europe. While traveling from Adrianople (now Edirne) to Constantinople (now İstanbul), de Busbecque saw "an abundance of flowers everywhere—narcissus, hyacinth, and those the Turks called *tulipam*—much to our astonishment because it was almost midwinter, a season unfriendly to flowers," according to an account he left.

Although the Turkish word for tulip is *lale*, his interpreter probably described the flower as looking like a *thoulypen,* the Turkish word for turban. De Busbecque probably heard "tulipam," which ultimately was shortened to "tulip." The Fleming bought some bulbs, "which cost me not a little," he noted. Upon returning to Vienna, he planted them in the Imperial gardens. They multiplied, word of their existence and beauty spread, and wealthy merchants in Holland soon coveted the new, prestigious flowers.

Although representations of tulips, particularly those that today are called "lily-flowering,"

*Fields of tulips in Holland during the blooming season create dazzling carpets of patchwork color throughout the country.*

appeared in Turkish fabric design hundreds of years ago, it was not until 1561 that the first accurate botanical drawing of a tulip appeared in Europe. Swiss botanist Konrad Gesner included one in a garden manual that he produced. Linnaeus, the renowned plant classifier, later named all garden tulips after him—*Tulipa gesneria.*

In 1593, Carolus Clusius, a Flemish botanist who had been Imperial gardener in Vienna, returned to Holland to chair the botany department at the University of Leiden. He brought with him a supply of tulips and planted them in his garden. Word spread and soon Clusius was besieged with extravagant offers for his prized specimens. According to one account, he decided to ask "such an exorbitant price that no one could procure them." But one night, while he slept, someone entered his garden and dug up and stole almost all of the tulips. A period document relates that the thief "wasted no time in increasing them by sowing seeds, and by this means, the seventeen provinces of Holland were well stocked."

But the romance of the tulip does not end here. New varieties of tulips occur when cultivated varieties "break," often unpredictably, producing new colors and markings. It has only been recently that scientists have concluded that these "breaks" are caused by a combination of natural mutation and a virus that spreads among the tulip bulbs. These new flamboyantly striped and wildly colored tulips were highly prized by the upper classes of the early-seventeenth-century Europe.

In 1624, according to a contemporary report, one bulb of 'Semper Augustus,' a red-and-white tulip with a base of a blue tinge, sold at auction for the equivalent of $1,200. The next year the owner sold two bulbs propagated from the first for $30,000. What has become known as "tulip mania" ensued, as all gardeners, rich and poor alike, realized that new varieties, which might lead to untold riches, could possibly be developed from any bulb in anybody's garden.

By 1654, the mania turned to madness, as bulb speculating tempted many. However, what was being traded were not bulbs, but bulb futures, the bulbs being sold often not having even bloomed yet. Men frantically mortgaged their houses and hocked the family jewels to raise money for tulip speculation. A brewer traded his brewery for one coveted bulb, and a miller, his mill. Meanwhile, at the University of Leiden, a botany professor named Evraard Forstius was so incensed by the exploitation that during his daily walks, he beat to death with his walking stick any tulip he encountered.

Then one spring day in 1637, three years after the start of the madness, the tulips market collapsed. A financial panic ensued, fortunes were lost, and some investors were driven to suicide. The government banned further tulip speculation and the Dutch turned to hybridizing and growing bulbs commercially as they continue to do today.

As new varieties were introduced, word of their beauty spread. The striped tulips, known as Rembrandts today, were popular with the Flemish and Dutch, to the point that the great masters of the period often included them on their canvases. The seventeenth-century French court, on the other hand, favored the fringed parrot tulips. The Darwin, named for Charles Darwin, was bred in the late 1880s in Haarlem by E. H. Krelage and Son. At the time, experts claimed it was not new at all, but the sturdy stems and square-shaped base ultimately were accepted as being new, and by 1892, the first Darwin tulip received "the only gold medal" at the Paris International Exhibition.

By the end of the eighteenth century, tulips were being used on the great estates of Europe and America. Even George Washington and Thomas Jefferson installed major plantings at Mount Vernon and Monticello, respectively. The American botanist John Bartram of Philadelphia, a colleague and friend of Benjamin Franklin and King George III's official "botanist for North America," was perhaps the first to actually import bulbs to the Western Hemisphere. Bartram, whose extensive correspondence with English botanist Peter Collinson has survived, received a supply of bulbs from Collinson in 1735. In 1739, Collinson sent some double tulips, and in 1740, "twenty varieties of crocus, some narcissus and ornithogalum." In 1763, Bartram received "thousands of bulbs" from his English friend. Today, Bartram's house is preserved as a museum and his Philadelphia garden, America's oldest surviving botanical garden, dating from 1728, is being restored.

In 1750, William Logan, son of James Logan, William Penn's secretary, planted hyacinths and tulips imported from England in his garden at Stenton, Pennsylvania, and in 1770, Daniel Wister of Grublethorpe, Germantown, was growing "beds of tulips" and "named" hyacinths. Wister's "beds of tulips" seem to have been the first in the New World.

According to available information, the first Dutchman to come to America specifically to sell flowering bulbs was J. B. van der Schoot. He traveled here for six months in 1840, selling Dutch bulbs to the people of New York, Philadelphia, Baltimore, Washington, Albany, and Buffalo. His descendants are still in the bulb business, under the name of W. R. van der Schoot Company.

Before 1850, only wild species of daffodils were available, many of the early immigrants having brought bulbs with them from Europe. After 1850, hybridization began, primarily in England. In 1899, 'King Alfred,' to this day the most popular of all the daffodil varieties, was introduced. During the 1920s, hybridization accelerated and the curtain went up on the modern daffodil. During that decade, 'Carbineer,' 'Carleton,' 'Trevithian' and 'Mrs. R. O. Backhouse' were introduced. It was also during the twenties that the bulb growers of Holland began to hybridize and grow daffodils for export.

Other bulbs, particularly the crocus and the lily, have their own romantic history. The ancient Minoans had discovered that the stigmas of the crocus that grew on the island could be pressed and an orange-yellow powder could be processed from it. This powder came to be called saffron, and it was the basis of the wealth of the Minoan civilization. Saffron was used as a spice, a dye, a scent, and a miracle drug by early medical men.

After the Minoan civilization vanished, saffron was used in many cultures as currency, almost as good as gold. It was not until the medieval era that the saffron crocus (*Crocus sativus*, an autumn-flowering crocus) reached England, where it was raised profitably by farmers in Essex. The ancient town of Saffron Walden, with its medieval marketplace, was the center of the English saffron trade.

These days, saffron is used mainly as a spice, particularly by the Spanish, who use it to create their national dish, arroz con pollo, or chicken with rice. It is very expensive, requiring the stigmas of four thousand crocuses to make one ounce of powder!

The lily is one of the oldest plants known to man. It has been inscribed on five-thousand-year-old Sumerian tablets and depicted in the art of every known civilization since. The Greeks used it as the symbol of Hera, and the Romans, of Juno. In Christian history, the white lily has come to symbolize the purity of the Virgin Mary.

And finally, hyacinths have appeared in literature and art since the Greek civilization. There are two mythological versions of their origin. In one the hyacinth sprang up where the blood of Ajax soaked the ground during the battle of Troy. In the other, the hyacinth grew from the blood of the boy Hyacinthus, who was accidentally killed by a discus thrown by Apollo. Hyacinths are native to the eastern Mediterranean area and to the Middle East, where they have been cultivated for thousands of years.

Although most of the bulbs we grow today are cultivated in Holland, the begonia industry is centered in Belgium. And of late, our own Pacific Northwest has become an important world center in the cultivation, hybridization, and commercial growing of lilies.

# *Chapter Two*

# GETTING STARTED

The word *bulb* is used to describe the category of plants that grow not from a root mass or from seed but from strange-looking, often twisted, masses of organic matter. In a general sense, it is used loosely to describe five different categories of plants: true bulbs, corms, tubers, tuberous roots, and rhizomes, each of which grows and stores food in slightly different ways.

Daffodils and tulips are *true bulbs*. One of nature's miracle packages, the bulb contains everything the plant needs to grow and flower. Within the bulb is the embryo of the plant, which is surrounded by growing matter that contains all of the food—starch, sugar, and some protein—necessary to nourish the plant. This is all held in place by the basal plate at the bottom of the bulb. When the plant starts to grow, roots emerge from the rim of this basal plate.

Crocuses and gladiolas grow from *corms*. The plants grow from the tops of the corm, from indentations called *eyes*. Beneath is the tissue that contains the food, and at the bottom of the corm is a basal plate. After the growing season, the corm is depleted, but new corms form on top of or around the basal plate.

*Tubers*, such as begonias and caladiums, have bumpy surfaces that sport many eyes, and it is from these that the shoots emerge. The food is stored in the mass of stem tissue contained in the tuber.

Dahlias grow from *tuberous roots*, the only category of bulb that houses food in a true root. The plant grows not from the roots but from eyes at the base of the plant's stem.

The last category is a *rhizome*. Calla and canna lilies and lily of the valley fit into this category. The plant grows from a horizontally growing root that has eyes on top and roots below. Shoots emerge from the eyes and the roots feed the plant from nutrients in the soil.

## BUYING BULBS

You're probably noticed that toward the end of summer and the beginning of fall, enormous banners advertising Dutch bulbs begin to appear at garden centers and nurseries, and even in some supermarkets. The fall season is the time to buy and plant tulips, daffodils, hyacinths, and other hardy spring-blooming bulbs.

The summer-blooming bulbs, almost all of which are tender (they do not survive winter temperatures in most parts of the country), are purchased in mid-spring, after the below-freezing temperatures of winter are over. The spring season, after all danger of frost is gone, is the time to plant almost all summer-blooming bulbs. Those summer bloomers that must have a head start on the season need to be started indoors in January or February. They include tuberous begonias, caladiums, and colocasia and are usually available locally in January or February.

Winter-blooming bulbs, which must be

*This assortment of ready-to-plant bulbs includes hyacinths, tulips, daffodils, crocus corms, and muscari.*

grown indoors as houseplants in most areas of the country, are available in late fall or during the winter at local florists, garden centers, or nurseries and through mail-order sources.

If you limit your bulb buying to local garden centers or nurseries, you may find that, more often than not, selection and sometimes supplies are limited. Many mail-order nurseries offer a wider selection; simply write for their free catalogues (see pages 144–45) and order. The time to write for catalogues for spring-blooming bulbs—those that you plant in the fall—is in July or early August. Decide what you want and place your order by the beginning of August. Mail-order sources usually offer the winter-blooming bulbs in the fall catalogue but deliver them at the appropriate time for your area. The time to write for catalogues for summer-blooming bulbs is in February or March. Decide what you want and place your order by the end of March. Almost all mail-order companies deliver bulbs at the proper planting time for your area. In this way, you will be assured of getting what you want and avoid the disappointment of desired varieties being sold out.

## CLIMATES SUITABLE FOR BULBS

Regardless of whether you are ordering bulbs for spring, summer, or fall, before you begin your selection, consult the plant hardiness zone map on page 8 to see which zone you live in, then check the zones at the beginning of each individual bulb entry to see if that particular bulb is recommended for your region.

Most mail-order catalogues include zone indications in their plant descriptions. Note that the very warm and cold areas of the United States and Canada are often inappropriate for some bulb varieties, particularly those that are planted in the fall and bloom in the spring. This is because most spring-blooming bulbs need a period of cold to develop roots, while others are too tender for extreme cold.

## SELECTING A SITE

The first thing to consider when choosing a site is light. Most spring-, summer-, and fall-blooming bulbs require either full or partial sun in order to perform well. Very few thrive in deep shade, so avoid areas under evergreen trees, foundations with northern exposures, and other areas that receive little sunlight. Check the individual entries for the specific light requirements of the bulbs you wish to plant and select a site on your property that is appropriate to their needs.

The second thing to consider is drainage. All spring- and fall-blooming bulbs and most of the summer-blooming bulbs, with the exception of some varieties of calla lilies, require good drainage to grow properly. Beyond the obvious—that is, avoid swampy soil or areas where water gathers and remains after rain—you can easily test a planting site for proper drainage by digging a hole the depth at which the bulbs will be planted—usually eight to twelve inches. Fill the hole with water and allow it to soak in. Repeat this two more times. After the third time, record how long it takes the water to sink in. If it takes more than six hours, the drainage is not sufficient for grow-

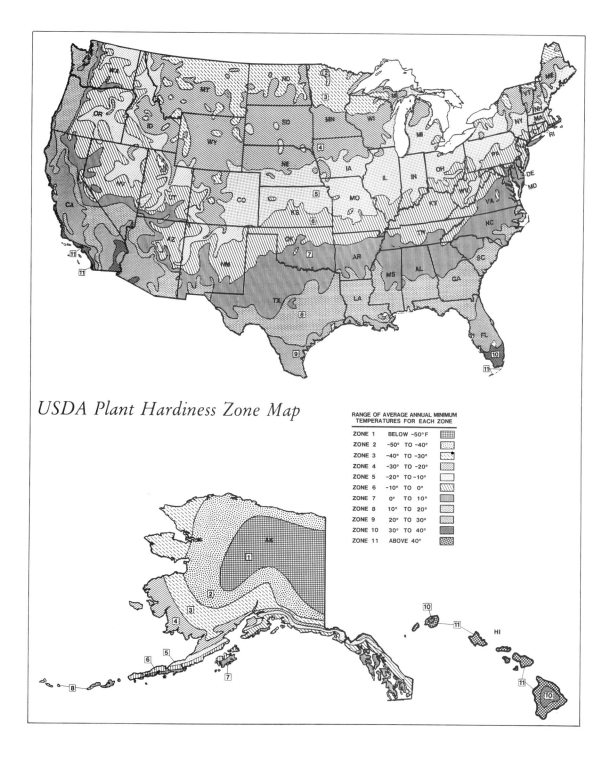

*USDA Plant Hardiness Zone Map*

RANGE OF AVERAGE ANNUAL MINIMUM
TEMPERATURES FOR EACH ZONE

| ZONE 1 | BELOW −50°F |
| ZONE 2 | −50° TO −40° |
| ZONE 3 | −40° TO −30° |
| ZONE 4 | −30° TO −20° |
| ZONE 5 | −20° TO −10° |
| ZONE 6 | −10° TO 0° |
| ZONE 7 | 0° TO 10° |
| ZONE 8 | 10° TO 20° |
| ZONE 9 | 20° TO 30° |
| ZONE 10 | 30° TO 40° |
| ZONE 11 | ABOVE 40° |

ing bulbs and you should select another site for the planting. Your bulbs will most likely rot in the location.

## PREPARATION OF SOIL

Once you have selected your site, you must prepare the soil. Soils range from very sandy and light to very heavy and clayey, differing not only from one part of the country to another but within any given area and, in fact, within a given property. If the soil lacks organic matter, and thus nutrients for the plants, success in growing bulbs will be quite limited. Therefore, whenever you install a bulb planting, or for that matter any kind of planting, it is a good idea to fortify and prepare the soil. While soil fortification does require some work, it will definitely help ensure good long-term results.

To prepare the soil, first place a drop cloth or large piece of heavy-duty plastic next to the bed. Excavate the planting area to a depth of at least one foot, placing the excavated soil on top of the drop cloth as you dig. This will help keep the surrounding area tidy and make the job of replacing the soil easier. Remove and dispose of all medium-size and large stones and other debris. Then mix the excavated soil with organic material in a ratio of two parts soil to one part organic material. You can use sphagnum peat moss, well-rotted manure, compost, or a combination of all three. Never use fresh manure, though, as it can burn tender roots. Mix the soil and organic material thoroughly using a shovel or your hands, and then shovel the mixture back into the excavated bed. Water thoroughly. It is best to do this several days in advance of your bulb planting.

## PLANTING OF BULBS

Once you have designed your spring, summer, or fall bulb scheme, purchased the bulbs, selected the appropriate site, and fortified the planting bed, it is time to plant. Bring a ruler so you can measure the appropriate depth and spacing of the bulbs. This information is included in each individual entry. Be sure you have your design scheme as well. You will also need some fertilizer. For many years it was universally thought that all-purpose 5-10-5 fertilizer and bone meal were the best foods for bulbs. However, recent research conducted by the Netherlands Flower Bulb Industry has revealed that adding bone meal is a waste of time and money. It is now thought that a fertilizer with a 9-9-6 ratio of nitrogen, phosphorus, and potassium ensures the best results. This fertilizer, called Holland Bulb Booster, is available at many nurseries and garden centers, as well as from mail-order supply houses.

As a general rule, you should dig a hole that is twice as deep as the recommended depth for a particular bulb. Mix the fertilizer with the soil in a ratio of one tablespoon per square foot, three-quarters of a cup per ten square feet, and four cups per fifty square feet. Replace the soil to the recommended planting level and flatten it by patting the bottom gently with your hand. This will ensure an even surface for the bulbs so they won't fall on their sides when you fill the hole with soil. Set the bulbs in place with their pointed ends up and gently press them into the soil. Cover the bulbs with the rest of the soil, tamp down lightly, and water thoroughly. If there are dry spells in your area during the fall or spring after planting spring- or summer-blooming bulbs, water the

*Drifts of* Iris reticulata *bulbs have been set in place in the rockery and are ready to cover with soil.*

planting thoroughly at least once a week throughout the whole dry season.

## INTERPLANTING AND OVERPLANTING

Although it would seem to be obvious, few but the most experienced gardeners are aware of the aesthetic advantages of interplanting and overplanting bulbs. This is the way you can enjoy continuous bloom throughout the spring season.

To interplant, select bulbs that require the same planting depth, then simply alternate them within any area. When finished, fill the hole to soil level and water thoroughly.

To overplant, plant early-blooming bulbs that require shallow planting depths over later-blooming bulbs that require slightly deeper planting. For example, place late-blooming tulip bulbs so that the tops of the bulbs are six inches below soil level. Then fill in the hole to a depth of two inches and plant early-blooming crocuses, galanthus, or eranthis. When finished, fill the hole to soil level and water thoroughly.

## CUTTING FLOWERS FOR ENJOYMENT INDOORS

Spring- and summer-flowering bulbs offer a profusion of cut flowers for indoor enjoyment. If you decide to pick a bouquet for your house, cut blooms that are neither fully open nor tight buds. It is best to select blossoms that are just beginning to open.

Cut the stems with a sharp knife and leave as much of the foliage on the plants as possible, since much of the food for the next year's growth is contained in this year's foliage.

It is best to cut flowers late in the afternoon, second best in early morning. Those cut in the heat of the day do not last very long. Once the flowers are cut, immerse the stems in a deep container filled with warm water (about 100° F) and leave in a cool location for several hours or, even better, overnight.

The next day, arrange them in your favorite container. Change the water and cut a little of the stem off every day to expose fresh cells for water absorption. If you place flowers out of direct sun in a cool spot, they will last longer.

## MAINTAINING YOUR BULBS

Each year after your initial planting of spring bulbs, when the bulbs begin to emerge from the ground in late winter or early spring, apply a dusting of 9-9-6 fertilizer (Holland Bulb Booster) at a rate of one tablespoon per square foot, three-quarters of a cup per ten square feet, and four cups per fifty square feet. Sprinkle the fertilizer evenly on the soil surface of the bulb planting.

After tulips, daffodils, hyacinths, and scilla bloom, cut off their spent flower stalks. Other bulb blossoms will wither and drop off naturally. Do *not* cut off the foliage of *any* type of bulb; the leaves contain substantial amounts of nutrients that are needed for next year's bloom. These nutrients are transported to the bulb, replenishing it. If you cut the foliage, you will rob the plant of its natural food supply for the next year. Allow the foliage to wither and dry naturally; then you can remove it. If you find the foliage unsightly, you can either tie it up in bundles with string or rubber bands, or overplant annuals or perennials in the area to hide it. See Chapter 3 for further ideas.

Remove weeds as they grow in any type of bulb planting, for they compete for available moisture and nutrients, as well as for light and space. Also, many pests, as well as some diseases, find shelter among the weeds. Although most bulbs are equipped to fight off pest and disease infestation, if they are choked by weeds they stand little chance of growing vigorously. To help control weeds, as well as to retain moisture, you might want to mulch your bulb plantings, especially summer-blooming bulbs, with a two- to three-inch layer of well-rotted compost, wood chips, or other mulching material.

## PROPAGATING BULBS

One of the many assets bulbs possess is the ability many of them have to multiply freely. So, with a little time and effort, over the years, you can increase your display of bloom throughout the year. Each one of the categories of bulbs—i.e., true bulbs, corms, tubers, tuberous roots, and rhizomes—multiplies in a different manner. Here's how you can propagate your own blooming stock.

*True bulbs:* After a number of years in the garden, true bulbs form a crowded mass beneath the soil surface. This is because the bulbs have multiplied and the planting is too crowded for proper growth and bloom. When this happens it is time to dig, separate, and replant the bulbs. You will know it is time to do this when bloom begins to diminish; this is particularly true of daffodils. After the bulb foliage has totally yellowed and withered, dig up the clump with a pitchfork. Try not to insert the fork too close to the planting, as this will result in sliced bulbs. In a shady place, remove the soil and separate all of the crowded bulbs and replant them immediately to avoid having the bulbs dry out. Plant larger bulbs in a permanent spot and smaller ones in a nursery to grow for several seasons until they reach flowering size. Then dig them up as described above and replant in a permanent spot.

*Corms:* In the case of hardy plants that grow from corms, such as crocus, digging and dividing may not be necessary for four or five years. However, gladiolas and acidanthera, tender summer bulbs that in most parts of the country must be dug up each fall and wintered indoors, can be divided each year. When the foliage has withered on hardy plants, dig up the planting, separate the cormels (small corms) that have formed around the plant, and carefully remove the new corm that has grown on top of the old ones. When the soil has dried, brush it off, place the corms in an open mesh vegetable bag or old nylon stocking, and store in a cool place (around 50° F). Replant in the fall.

The same process is followed to propagate the tender summer bulbs. In this case, however, dig the corms when the foliage has withered or late in fall before the first frost. Cut off the top foliage and dry for two or three weeks in a shady frost-free place on a screen or in open trays. Once the corms are dry, remove the soil on them and separate them as described above. The small cormels can be planted in the holding garden and grown for several years, until they are ready to flower and be transferred to their permanent planting.

*Tubers:* An entirely different method is used to propagate plants that grow from tubers, such as caladiums, tuberous begonias, and gloriosa lilies. Like their potato cousins, these tubers have buds, which are called eyes, scattered all over their surface. Each of these eyes will produce a shoot, which in turn will produce a flowering plant. In the spring, before planting, cut the tuber with a sharp knife, making sure that each section has at least one large bud or eye. Then dust the cut surface with a fungicide powder, available at garden centers and nurseries. Let the pieces dry for two days in a warm, dry, shady spot, and then plant them.

*Tuberous roots:* Dahlias are included in this category of bulbs. Whereas the eyes on tubers are scattered across their entire surface, the eyes on tuberous rooted plants are concentrated in one place, at the base of the original stem. You will notice that dahlias have a collection of elongated, chubby roots. These roots have no eyes. To propagate, cut the root system into pieces, making sure that *each* piece has a portion of the original stem on it. Dust cuts with a fungicide powder, let pieces dry for two days in a warm, dry, shady spot, and then plant them.

*Rhizomes:* The rhizomes of calla lilies, canna lilies, and lilies of the valley can also be propagated to create more plants. The rhizomes are thick stems that grow horizontally near the surface of the soil; the roots grow down into the soil and the eyes are on the top. Divide with a knife, being sure that each segment contains at least one eye. Dust cuts with a fungicide powder, let pieces dry for two days in a warm, dry, shady spot, and then plant them.

# WINTER PROTECTION

Since most summer bulbs are tender and are planted in the spring, after all danger of frost is past, and dug up before the first frost, in autumn or winter, outdoor protection is not necessary. Tender bulbs are wintered indoors, each genus requiring a different kind of preparation and storage treatment. See individual entries for further information.

Since spring-blooming bulbs are hardy, a winter mulch is not necessary in most areas of the country. However, in the far northern climates, USDA zones 2 and 3, it is a good idea to apply a six-inch layer of salt hay, available at garden centers and nurseries, over the planting after the first deep frost. Remove this mulch in late winter or early spring, when the bulbs first begin to emerge from the ground.

Keep in mind that, in many parts of the country, spring-blooming bulbs will begin to send up shoots in January or February, sometimes even through snow. Do not worry, they are hardy and will not be damaged by subsequent cold snaps.

# PESTS AND DISEASES

Although spring- and fall-flowering bulbs and most summer-flowering bulbs are virtually insect- and disease-free, most are not animal- or rodent-proof. The bulbs and foliage of daffodils and narcissi and most scilla are poisonous to animals and rodents, so they do not nibble these either above or below ground. However, most other bulbs are taste treats for deer, raccoons, rabbits, chipmunks, and burrowing creatures, such as moles and voles. Check the individual bulb entries that follow for more specific information.

If deer and raccoons are a problem, the best thing to do, beyond building fences, is to sprinkle dried blood meal on the shoots when they emerge (they dislike the smell). You'll have to reapply it after each rain. Dried blood meal is available at most garden centers, nurseries, and through mail-order sources. It also serves as a fertilizer for the plants.

Rabbits and chipmunks find tulips and crocuses particularly delectable. Late in the winter, when food is scarce for these animals, the fresh young shoots make a gourmet meal for them. As soon as you see shoots emerging, sprinkle a handful of dried blood meal on and around the foliage, and do so after every rain. If rabbits and chipmunks still nibble, place a handful of mothballs here and there among the plantings.

If the problem is severe, I have found that placing a piece of one-inch-mesh chicken wire over the entire planting helps keep creatures away. Once the emerging shoots are several inches tall, rabbits and chipmunks don't seem to savor them, so I remove the chicken wire.

Moles burrow beneath the ground, eating the grubs that live beneath the surface and feeding on grass or weed roots and some bulbs. You'll know if this is your problem because attacked areas have a spongy feel when walked upon and often you can see the surface soil crumbled and raised up above the surrounding soil level. If you can rid your lawn of grubs, the moles will probably follow. There are insecticides available at garden centers and nurseries that you can apply to your lawn to kill grubs. Check with your county cooperative extension service for information about which insecticides are recommended and/or permitted in your area.

There is an added complication with moles: They burrow holes into the beds and then voles, tailless creatures that look like field mice, follow behind them and clean out bulb plantings. One of my neighbors, particularly plagued with a vole problem, told me of sitting in his tulip garden one afternoon with friends and, right before their very eyes, seeing a tulip in full bloom slowly sink into the ground and disappear. The vole below had gotten a hold on the bulb and was pulling it through the burrow.

There are many homegrown solutions to the vole problem. Some people suggest placing Juicy Fruit gum in the holes, others say dead fish. I've tried dozens of these "solutions" and still the voles cleaned out the bulb plantings. While traveling in northern Portugal, I visited the beautiful gardens at the Quinta de Aveleda and noticed the telltale spongy mounds on the grass surface. I spoke with Antonio Guedes, the knowledgeable owner of the garden, and he told me that to pro-

*Two ways to protect bulbs from moles and voles are to set bulbs in pots and sink them into the ground or to line the excavated planting area with wire mesh before setting the bulbs in place.*

tect his bulbs from moles and voles, he places a series of plastic containers in a given bed, puts some drainage material, such as pebbles, in the bottom of each, and then sets the bulbs inside the pots. I have tried this and it works well with the small "minor" bulbs, but tulips bloomed only once using this method.

As a result of many years' experience, I have found that the best way to outsmart the critters is to dig the bed for the bulbs and then line the entire bed with the flexible, soft wire mesh used for keeping leaves out of rain gutters on the eaves of a house. This material is available in hardware stores. I have a planting, now in its fourth year, of *speciosum* lilies, particularly savored by burrowing creatures, that I installed in a wire-lined bed. This system seems to work.

I suggest that you inquire locally at nurseries and garden centers or at your local cooperative extension service to find out if there is a vole and mole problem in your area. If it is serious, run a trial planting of a few bulbs to see if the burrowing rodents are present and hungry before you install a large and expensive unprotected planting. I have a neighbor who installed over a thousand tulips without doing any prior testing—not one survived to bloom the following spring!

If the problem is very serious, and for one reason or another you are not prepared to construct a protective wire-mesh shield, plant only spring-blooming daffodils and scilla, which are impervious to animal damage.

## *Chapter Three*

# LANDSCAPING WITH BULBS

You can install a bulb planting virtually anywhere you want spring, summer, or a little fall color. Here are some places that work particularly well:

- In flower beds
- In flower or shrub borders
- Interplanted among foundation plantings
- Along driveways
- Along walks
- In rock gardens
- In the midst of ground covers such as creeping myrtle, ajuga, pachysandra, or ivy
- At the foot of walls
- Naturalized in the lawn

*Masses of daffodils planted beneath spring-flowering trees come up year in and year out, multiplying and becoming more lush with each passing spring.*

- In front of evergreen hedges
- Along fences
- Around mailboxes
- Around birdbaths, sundials, or other garden ornaments
- Naturalized in fields, under deciduous trees, or in woods
- In containers on patios or terraces
- In distant stretches of your property
- In a dooryard garden—particularly effective with spring-blooming bulbs, some of which provide color from midwinter into early spring
- In window boxes. If you opt for a spring-blooming window box, plant the bulbs up in pots in the fall and sink them into the ground in the garden. In early spring, remove the pots from the garden and transfer the bulbs to the window boxes. Spring-blooming bulbs will rot if they spend the winter in a window box.

If you are going to invest your time and money in a large-scale bulb planting, you will want it to be in harmony with your landscape and to add beauty to your home and surroundings. Although rules are made to be broken, in general, here are a few design basics you can apply to spring-, summer-, and fall-flowering bulbs.

• When planting the major spring-blooming bulbs (tulips, standard daffodils, hyacinths, and Dutch crocuses) always set them out in groups of at least twelve, or their impact will be greatly diminished. It is best to plant twenty-four if your budget permits. "Minor" bulbs should be planted in groups of no less than fifty, preferably a hundred, or they, too, will be lost.

• Always plant at least six of the same variety of lilies, three of the same variety of dahlias, begonias, and caladiums, and twelve of most of the other summer-blooming bulbs, such as gladiola, acidanthera, tigridia, etc.

• Never buy a rainbow mixture of bulbs. The result at bloom time will be a hodgepodge of color, ineffective and often messy-looking.

• Avoid planting bulbs in a straight line or in a single circle around a tree or bush—the result will be thin and unnatural-looking.

• When planning a bulb scheme, concentrate on two or three colors in each location but do not mix them together. For example, a cluster or drift of violet-colored tulips next to a drift of yellow and another of white looks more harmonious than one cluster each of violet, orange, red, pink, yellow, and white.

• Decide whether you want a formal- or informal-looking bulb garden and then stick to your decision. Keep in mind that an informal garden is asymmetrical and is thus more appropriate for the majority of residences. Few of us live in houses that are so stately that a formal planting is called for.

• Hyacinths and certain tulips—tall Darwin, lily-flowering, cottage, triumph, and Darwin hybrid—are stately and somewhat rigid in appearance, so use them sparingly unless you want a very formal look. Species tulips, daffodils, and the "minor" bulbs are often better suited to an informal planting.

• Lilies, dahlias, and other summer-blooming bulbs look best when interplanted with perennials, annuals, or shrubs. The stems and foliage of many summer-blooming bulbs, particularly lilies, are rigid and become unsightly after bloom. It is a good idea to overplant medium-height annuals, such as marigolds or zinnias or cleomes, on the lily bed, or to interplant daylilies. The foliage of the daylilies and their long blooming period will hide the rigid, unsightly lily foliage and add color to the area once the lilies have finished blooming.

• Consider the landscape not only from the outdoor point of view, but also based on how it will look from indoors, through windows. Since bulbs begin blooming in late February and continue on through the spring, arrange your outdoor plantings of early-blooming bulbs so that you can enjoy them from inside as well as outside. Chances are that with late winter and early spring cold and rain, you won't be spending too much time outdoors soaking in the floral display.

• For displays in distant parts of your property, plant large groups of a single variety of bulbs in drifts rather than in symmetrical beds. The effect is more natural-looking and eye-catching.

• When buying bulbs, be sure you buy healthy ones. Here are a few things to look for: If ordering from a mail-order source, order only from reputable firms, some of which appear in the Appendix. This does not mean that sources not listed are not reputable, just that those that are listed can be trusted. If you are buying bulbs at a garden center or nursery, use your eyes. Look to see

*The soft mauve blossoms and variegated foliage of lamium, along with the brilliant yellow of coreopsis, set off this planting of hybrid lilies.*

order bulb suppliers offer mixtures of daffodils for naturalizing at reduced prices. These are certainly worth the money if you plan to naturalize them in meadows, woods, or under deciduous trees. The other exception is end-of-season sales at nurseries and garden centers. Individual varieties of bulbs are often reduced in price toward the middle of November. Since there is still time to plant, you might wish to consider buying some of these to fill in your landscape after your initial planting. However, don't avail yourself of these bargains when installing your initial bed; the selection is usually quite limited and has been well picked over.

## PLANNING YOUR BULB PLANTING

Always design your planting on graph paper first. Obtainable from most stationery and office supply stores, graph paper is divided by lines into one-inch-square blocks; those blocks are further divided into smaller squares, usually six to an inch. Use a scale of one small block on the paper to two inches of garden space and sketch out the area you wish to plant. This means that a single one-inch block on the paper is equal to one square foot in the garden. Not only will this method assure that you purchase enough bulbs for your planting, but since the foliage of spring-blooming bulbs withers and dies by summer, you will always have a record of exactly where you have installed a bulb planting, information of great importance in the likely event that you'll later want to fill in the planting with annuals or interplant

if the bulbs are healthy-looking, free of mildew or disease, unbruised, and without blemishes. Then feel them. If they are firm and not soft or mushy, have no soft spots, and are heavy in relation to their size, they should be healthy.

• Although not of an aesthetic nature, this tip will prove invaluable: *Beware of bargains!* Bulbs are quite inexpensive in the first place, and bargain collections sometimes include bulbs of inferior quality. As a rule, you get what you pay for. There are, however, two exceptions. Many mail-

*To enjoy early-blooming bulbs during the cold, nasty late winter days, be sure to plant some within view or along the path to the mailbox or garage. Here are species tulips and deep blue* Scilla siberica.

and overplant with perennials. With this record you will avoid digging up or slicing any bulbs with a shovel or spade as you install new plants or move others.

Another way to mark your bulb plantings is to insert plastic or metal markers, available at garden centers or nurseries or through mail-order sources. I have found that although the plastic markers serve well for a year or two, eventually they become brittle and break. Do not use wooden markers; they will rot within a year. When you write the name of the species or cultivar on the label, be sure to use a pen with in-

delible ink or a soft-lead pencil. Yet another way to mark plantings is to paint the tops of large aluminum nails, those used for installing rain gutters on houses, in different colors with oil-based enamel paints coded for your plantings, and sink them into the ground in the planting.

*These pale pink-and-white 'Angelique' peony tulips are underplanted with a stand of delicate, pale blue forget-me-nots and set off by the pale pinks of English daisies, creating a particularly subtle color combination.*

These are relatively inconspicuous.

In any event, do not trust your memory—although you may think you will remember what is what and where it is, you probably won't.

Here are a few pointers to help you plan your garden:

• Tall-growing bulbs are generally best placed to the rear of the bed, with medium-height bulbs in the middle and shorter ones to the front.

• White flowering bulbs are essential to break up color patterns. At least one-fourth of your bulb planting should be white.

• Have a color scheme in mind. Blue, purple, and pink interspersed with white and an occasional red is one suggestion. Blue, white, and yellow with an occasional purple or red and yellow and white with an occasional blue are other possibilities. Experiment with colors by using a paint box to see which combinations please you. As a rule, orange is an extremely difficult color to use in a flowering border; it is very bright and will dominate the scheme. For that reason, most experienced gardeners avoid it.

• If you plan to intersperse perennials or annuals in a spring or summer bulb border, consider their foliage colors as a backdrop to and filler between the brilliant colors of the bulbs. If a certain annual or perennial sports a beautiful flower but its foliage is a problematic color or ugly, avoid it. Most plants bear flowers for only a short period, while foliage, with few exceptions, is present all during the season.

• When you are ready to plant, take your chart with you to the garden and use it as a guide. Avoid last-minute changes, for they are almost always dead wrong.

# BLOOM SEQUENCE

Plan your plantings so that you have an extended sequence of bloom. Remember to interplant and overplant bulbs to further enhance a display (see page 10 on how to do this). In mail-order catalogues, you often see beautiful photographs of "collections" of bulbs, all in bloom at the same time. Outdoors, in your garden, this cannot happen. Crocuses bloom very early in the spring season and tulips bloom late in the spring season. The flowering bulb plants in the photographs have all been forced indoors to bring them into bloom at the same time. Some bulbs will overlap in their blooms—check the following sequences charts for them.

## Spring Bloom Sequence

Below is a chart of approximate blooming dates for various bulbs in the warmer areas of zones 5 and 6 and the colder areas of zone 7. If you live in zone 4, add one week; in zone 3, add about two weeks. In zone 8, subtract one week. Although you need to bear in mind that these dates are only approximate, they will help you in planning a sequence of bloom.

| BULB | BLOOM TIME |
| --- | --- |
| Crocus (Species) | March 1–20 |
| *Eranthis* (Winter aconite) | March 1–20 |
| *Galanthus* (Snowdrop) | March 1–20 |

| BULB | BLOOM TIME |
|---|---|
| *Iris danfordiae* | March 1–20 |
| *I. reticulata* | March 1–20 |
| *Bulbocodium vernum* | March 10–25 |
| Crocus (Dutch) | March 10–25 |
| *Chionodoxa* (Glory-of-the-snow) | March 25–April 10 |
| Daffodil (Early blooming) | March 25–April 10 |
| *Puschkinia scilloides* (Striped squill) | March 25–April 10 |
| *Anemone blanda* | April 1–15 |
| Tulip (Species) | April 1–30 |
| *Muscari* | April 10–25 |
| *Scilla siberica* | April 10–25 |
| Daffodil and narcissi | April 10–May 7 |
| *Hyacinthus orientalis* (Dutch hyacinth) | April 15–30 |
| *Fritillaria imperialis* | April 15–30 |
| *Scilla tubergeniana* | April 20–25 |
| *Fritillaria meleagris* | April 25–May 10 |
| *F. michailovskyi* | April 25–May 10 |
| Tulip: Darwin hybrid | April 25–May 10 |
| Tulip: Double peony | April 25–May 10 |
| Tulip: Early | April 25–May 10 |
| Tulip: Lily-flowering | April 25–May 10 |
| Tulip: Mendel | April 25–May 10 |
| Tulip: Triumph | April 25–May 10 |
| *Convallaria* (Lily of the valley) | May 1–15 |
| *Erythronium* | May 1–15 |
| *Ipheion* (Spring starflower) | May 1–15 |
| Iris (Dutch) | May 1–15 |
| *Leucojum* (Snowflake) | May 1–15 |
| *Ornithogalum umbellatum* (Star-of-Bethlehem) | May 1–15 |
| *Camassia* (Wild hyacinth) | May 5–20 |
| *Eremurus* (Foxtail lily) | May 5–20 |

| BULB | BLOOM TIME |
|---|---|
| Tulip: Cottage | May 5–20 |
| Tulip: Darwin | May 5–20 |
| Tulip: Parrot | May 5–20 |
| *Hyacinthoides (Scilla) hispanica* | May 15–30 |
| *Allium* | May 25–June 15 |

## Summer Bloom Sequence

Since summer bloomers are planted after all danger of frost has passed, there is a slight variation across the various zones in blooming dates. Still, because of the warm summer weather, bloom time is much the same throughout the country.

| BULB | BLOOM TIME |
|---|---|
| *Caladium* | Early summer to fall |
| *Colocasia* (Elephant's ear) | Early summer to fall |
| *Oxalis* | Early summer to fall |
| Tuberous begonia | Early summer to fall |
| *Agapanthus africanus* | Early to midsummer |
| *Anemone* | Early to midsummer |
| *Ranunculus asiaticus* | Early to midsummer |
| *Lilium* | Early to late summer, depending on variety |
| *Canna* | Midsummer |
| *Gloriosa* (Glory lily) | Midsummer |
| *Hymenocallis* (Spider lily) | Midsummer |
| *Ornithogalum thrysoides* | Midsummer |
| *Sparaxis* (Harlequin flower) | Midsummer |
| *Zephyranthes* (Fairy lily) | Midsummer |
| *Gladiolus* | Midsummer to fall |
| *Crocosmia* | Mid- to late summer |
| *Trigridia pavonia* | Mid- to late summer |
| *Zantedeschia* (Calla lily) | Mid- to late summer |
| *Polianthes tuberosa* | Late summer |
| *Acidanthera bicolor* | Midsummer to fall |
| *Dahlia* | Midsummer to fall |

## Fall Bloom Sequence

| BULB | BLOOM TIME |
|---|---|
| *Lycoris* (Spider lily) | Late summer, early fall |
| *Colchicum* (Meadow saffron) | Early to mid-fall |
| Crocus (Autumn blooming) | Early to mid-fall |
| Cyclamen (Species) | Early to mid-fall |

## Indoor Bloom Sequence

| BULB | BLOOM TIME |
|---|---|
| *Hippeastrum* (Amaryllis) | Early winter |
| *Narcissus tazetta* (Paperwhite) | Early winter |
| Cyclamen (Florist) | Early to late winter |
| *Freesia* | Early to late winter |
| All forced tulips, daffodils, crocuses, hyacinths, etc. | Mid- to late winter |
| *Sprekelia formosissima* | Mid- to late winter |
| *Clivia* (Kaffir lily) | Late winter to early spring |
| *Lachenalia* (Cape cowslip) | Late winter to early spring |
| *Crinum* | Grows in late winter and spring, blooms in summer |
| *Vallota speciosa* (Scarborough lily) | Grows in late winter, blooms in late spring and summer |

# COLOR IN YOUR GARDEN

Much has been written about planning a garden that is harmonious in color. To help you do this, I have provided you with some very basic guidelines.

The color wheel consists of the three primary colors—red, blue, and yellow—and the three secondary colors—purple, green, and orange.

They are placed this way around the wheel:

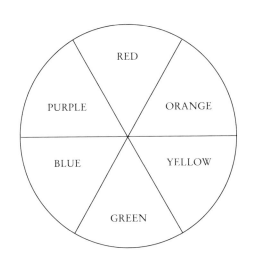

Note that the secondary colors are adjacent to the primary colors on the wheel and that accent colors, those that contrast nicely, are opposite the primary color on the wheel. Also keep in mind that when a color is specified, it means all shades of the color—in the case of red, that would include pink, carmine, scarlet, etc.

| PRIMARY GARDEN COLOR | SECONDARY GARDEN COLORS | ACCENT COLOR |
|---|---|---|
| Red | Purple and orange | Green |
| Purple | Blue and red | Yellow |
| Blue | Purple and green | Orange |
| Green | Blue and yellow | Red |
| Yellow | Green and orange | Purple |
| Orange | Yellow and red | Blue |

When you plan your color scheme, if you select purple as your main color, concentrate on using the adjacent secondary colors on the wheel—that is, red and blue, along with white when you select blossom color. This could include not only red but pink and mauve, and not only blue but lavender, light blue, deep blue, etc. An occasional accent can be provided by the opposite color on the wheel—in this case, yellow. This could be pale yellow or bright yellow, depending on your taste.

*'Red Riding Hood' Greigii tulips and white 'Jeanne d'Arc' Dutch crocus are interplanted and wake up the early spring garden from its winter rest.*

*Both blue* (Muscari armeniacum) *and white* (M.a. 'Album') *grape hyacinth are interplanted here, along with sky blue glory-of-the-snow* (Chionodoxa), *offering a color combination soothing to the eyes.*

Always keep in mind, though, that all rules are made to be broken. If you feel like mixing what appear to be incongruous colors, go ahead and do it. A number of years ago I installed a rhododendron and deciduous azalea garden accented with lilies. I had purchased unlabeled, hybridized rhodos and azaleas from the family of a gardener friend of mine who had passed away. That was before I learned that one never installs any plants in a permanent location without knowing the color of the blossoms and the growing habits of the plants. As it turned out, the rhododendron blossoms were in shades of purple, mauve, and pink, and the deciduous azaleas were in pale and bright oranges and salmons. The lilies I had planted were orange, sulphur yellow, and white.

A friend came to visit while the garden was in bloom. She was by education and profession an art historian. When I took her out to show her the garden I said, "It's all wrong, you know. I have to move the orange azaleas out and change the lily color scheme." At this point she screamed, "It's perfect! Don't change a thing! It's pure Gauguin!" And sure enough, as I looked, the colors were right off a Gauguin canvas. So now, when the garden is in bloom and I take visitors out to see it, I merely say—and indeed smugly, with just the right touch of pretentiousness—"This is my Gauguin garden!"

Point being, if you want to try an offbeat color combination, by all means do. You might find that it works for you.

What follows are some combinations suggested by the Netherlands Flower Bulb Information Center.

## BLUES AND YELLOWS

Combine shades of blue and yellow—color casts can range from pale yellow to deep gold, sky blue to turquoise. These pairings are used to best advantage in the garden when one color is selected as the principal shade and the other is used for accent.

• Deep blue grape hyacinths make a rich carpet against which to show off sulphur-yellow 'Monte Carlo,' a double early tulip. To extend the golden glow, add patches of a late-blooming golden trumpet narcissus such as 'Dutch Master.'
• Electrify a tall, robust planting of rich blue *Camassia quamash* with small clusters of all-yellow 'Carlton' trumpet narcissus.
• Add a rich accent of electric blue 'Blue Spike' *Muscari armeniacum* to any planting of yellow or gold daffodils.

*Here, electric blue* Scilla siberica *are interplanted with early-blooming miniature daffodil 'Tete-a-tete,' creating an effective color contrast.*

## RED AND YELLOW

Although many people find this combination garish, it is still the most popular color combination for bulbs in America, as well as worldwide.

*The deep red of 'Fireball' provides startling contrast to the bright yellow of 'Vanessa' and its paler cousin 'French Vanilla' in this lovely planting of hybrid lilies.*

• Plant drifts of 'Carioca' Greigii tulips, with their brilliant yellow blossoms and carmine-red outer petal markings, with white patches of the daisylike 'Bridesmaid' *Anemone blanda.*

• Pale yellow 'Ice Follies' daffodils and 'Red Emperor' tulips both bloom in April and offer a toned-down version of the yellow-and-red combination.

• Brilliant 'Red Riding Hood' Greigii tulips and bright yellow 'King Alfred' daffodils serve to wake up any spring garden from its long winter sleep.

• For a May display that will knock the socks off anyone, combine groups of tall-growing Darwin hybrid tulips—'Yellow Dover,' red-tinged yellow 'Queen Wilhelmina,' and bright red 'General Eisenhower' should satisfy any appetite for spectacle.

• Drifts of mid-season Triumph tulips—yellow-and-red 'Golden Mirjoran' and glowing scarlet 'Bing Crosby'—can be complemented with a foreground planting of yellow 'City of Haarlem' hyacinths.

## *PASTELS*

Pinks, corals, creams, lavenders, and other pastel shades are all available to the spring bulb gardener. Set amid the lush greens of spring, these soft hues and shades are pleasing to the eye.

• Match peony-flowered 'Lilac Perfection,' a late double tulip, with early-blooming perennial pink astilbe or a delicate pink forget-me-not. Deep velvety purple or maroon pansies make a good accent.

• The soft coral tones of 'Apricot Beauty' combine well with the soft pink of 'Peach Blossom' double-flowered tulips. These can be mixed with the taller, pink-hued large-cup narcissus known as 'Roseworthy.'

• 'Gander's Rhapsody,' a single late tulip, is lovely, with its bluish white cupped blossom blushed with melting rosy hues. Pair it with pale salmon-pink hyacinth 'Lady Derby' against a white-flowering shrub, such as spiraea, or a pink-flowering shrub, such as a deutzia or flowering almond.

*The soft pink pastel of 'Angelique' tulips is complemented effectively by the deep color of 'Scotch Lassie' Darwins in this May-blooming spectacle in a raised planter.*

## SHADES OF WHITE

For an understated bulb planting, perhaps merely to set off a lovely azalea, rhododendron, or dogwood setting, pure white and pale yellow are especially effective.

• Group 'White Pearl' hyacinths with 'Ice Follies' daffodils. Add a drift of pristine ' Purissima,' a white Fosteriana tulip.
• Pair 'Salome,' a white-and-salmon large-cup narcissus, with pure white grape hyacinth (*Muscari armeniacum* 'Album').
• Combine white 'Stainless' large-cup narcissus with 'Carnegie' white hyacinths and creamy ivory-yellow 'City of Haarlem' hyacinths.

## ORANGE AND PINK

Orange is one of the most difficult colors to use effectively in the garden; however, when combined with pink, it loses its glaring quality.

• Flame-colored 'Orange Emperor' Fosteriana tulips and creamy salmon-orange 'Gypsy Queen' hyacinths are stunning when offset by pink daisylike 'Charmer' *Anemone blanda*. Salmon-pink 'Apricot Beauty,' a single early tulip, adds a shimmering touch.
• 'General de Wet,' a delicate coral-orange single early tulip, is eye-catching with silvery white 'Pax,' a Triumph tulip, and pink 'Pink Pearl' or carmine-red 'Jan Bos' hyacinths.
• For an elegant touch, mix clusters of tall rose-hued 'Mariette' lily-flowering tulips with pure 'White Triumphator' lily-flowering tulips and 'Blushing Beauty,' a velvety yellow-and-apricot lily-flowering tulip.

*Crocuses naturalized in a woodland setting provide a spectacle of color in an otherwise dreary landscape.*

## PURPLE AND YELLOW

This color combination has always been a favorite for the spring and Easter season. Beyond the suggestions below, many others are possible. Glance through fall bulb catalogues for more ideas.

• Combine purple, yellow, and white crocuses in a concentrated planting for an early spring spectacle.
• Bright yellow 'West Point,' a lily-flowering

tulip, looks especially striking against a backdrop of purple or orchid azaleas.

• Deep velvety purple or burgundy-colored tulips are stunning in front of bushy lime-yellow euphorbia.

## *PURPLE OR BLUE AND BRIGHT RED*

For a touch of drama and the unexpected, combine bright red with purple or blue.

• A large drift of 'Blue Giant' *Hyacinthoides (Scilla) hispanica* overplanted with white-and-magenta 'Sorbet' single late tulips is very effective.

• Magenta 'Electra,' a double early tulip, with deep purple or violet-blue companion plantings of pansies or 'Blue Magic' hyacinths is stunning.

• The native perennial plant *Mertensia virginica* (Virginia bluebells) combines nicely with red 'Emperor' tulips.

• A drift of blue muscari overplanted on a bed of deep bluish purple 'King of the Blues' hyacinth interplanted with mahogany-red 'Cassini' Triumph tulips offers a mysterious color touch to a garden.

## *THE MIXED SPRING BULB GARDEN*

In general, you cannot complement a spring-blooming bulb garden with annuals because most are tender and will not tolerate late frosts. However, biennial pansy plants, usually available at garden centers in late March in six-packs, are frost tolerant and can be used.

There are, however, many early-blooming shrubs and perennials that can be used in tandem with spring-blooming bulbs.

If you look at the bulb sequence chart on pages 22–24, you will note that the earliest bulbs are the "minor" ones. These include:

| BULB | COLOR |
| --- | --- |
| *Bulbocodium vernum* | Pale lavender |
| Crocus (Dutch) | White, gold, deep purple, lavender |
| Crocus (Species) | White, cream, yellow, lilac, light blue, purple |
| *Eranthis* (Winter aconite) | Yellow |
| *Galanthus* (Snowdrop) | White |
| *Iris danfordiae* | Yellow |
| *I. reticulata* | Purple, light and medium blue |
| Miniature daffodil (early) | Yellow, gold |

The very earliest blooming bulbs, yellow winter aconite and white snowdrops, usually must stand alone in the garden, for there are no perennials that bloom as early as they do. The only shrubs that might bloom are *Magnolia stellata*, a white-flowering shrub of medium height, and the various early-blooming witch hazels. However, the bark of a white birch or a red-twig dogwood or any planting of evergreen shrubs or ground cover will enhance the tiny blooms of these early bloomers. If you decide you want an early display of these, they look lovely interplanted. Since their blooms are small, a substantial planting is called for in order to make some kind of statement. Plant not less than one hundred of each, preferably five hundred of each, and leave them, undisturbed, to multiply.

The next bulbs to bloom in the spring sequence are *Iris danfordiae, I. reticulata,* and the species crocus. There may well be some overlap-

*In this most unusual planting, photographed in Holland, the feathery, bright green foliage of these woodland ferns provides an extraordinary visual contrast to the jade green, spearlike foliage and bright yellow blossoms of these miniature daffodils.*

ping with the earlier blooming bulbs. *Magnolia stellata* will still be in bloom at this period, and pansies can be planted in front of, behind, or in between the emerging bulb shoots. At this time of year, we yearn for sparkling and somewhat striking color combinations; the purple of *I. reticulata* with the yellow *I. danfordiae* and perhaps white species crocus makes a good combination. Yellow pansies, or even pink ones,

would dress up an early bulb planting nicely.

As the season progresses, more early-blooming perennials flower and can be used to great advantage in a garden with bulbs. What follows on page 32 is a list of some of the most readily available perennials that will combine well with early-blooming spring bulbs. These all bloom in March and April in most parts of the country, with some still blooming in May.

The very earliest are marked with an asterisk(*).

All perennials can be planted in the fall when you install your bulbs or, if need be, in the spring. If you wish to overplant early blooming bulbs with perennials, it is best to plant both in the fall.

You might think, as you study the list, that a planting of bright yellow species crocus installed next to *Pulmonaria* 'Mrs. Moon,' with its

| PERENNIAL | DESCRIPTION | HEIGHT |
|---|---|---|
| *Aethionema* x *warleyense* (Warley rose) | Pink | 1–1½′ |
| *Alyssum saxatile* | Brilliant sulphur yellow | 12–15″ |
| *A.* 'Citrinum' | Pale yellow | 6–12″ |
| *A.* 'Sunny Border Apricot' | Apricot | 12–15″ |
| *Anemone pulsatilla** | White, red, or purple bell-shaped blossoms | 1–1½′ |
| *Arabis** | Mounds of clusters of white blossoms | 6″ |
| *Armeria* (Thrift)* | Mounds of deep rose-pink pincushion-shaped blossoms | 8″ |
| *Asperula* (Sweet woodruff) | Small, white blossoms | 3–6″ |
| *Aubrieta* (Rock cress)* | Mounds of various shades of purple, blue, or white blossoms | 6–10″ |
| *Brunnera macrophylla* | Blue forget-me-not–like blossoms | 1–1½′ |
| *Dicentra eximia* | Pink pantaloon-shaped blossoms | 1–1½′ |
| *Doronicum** | Bright yellow daisy-shaped blossoms | 1½–2′ |
| *Draba sibirica** | Tiny yellow flowers | 1″ |
| *Echeveria* (Hens and chicks)* | Succulent foliage of pink, green, jade, purple, or red | 1–3″ |
| *Helleborus orientalis* (Lenten rose)* | Pink blossoms | 12–18″ |
| *Iberis* (Candytuft)* | Clusters of low-growing white flowers | 8–12″ |
| *Lamium maculatum* | Clusters of white flowers | 6″ |
| *Mertensia virginica* (Virginia bluebells) | Blue bell-shaped blossoms | 1–2′ |
| *Primula** (Primrose) | Yellow, rust, red, pink, blue, purple, or combinations thereof | 6–12″ |
| *Pulmonaria angustifolia* | Blue blossoms | 9″ |
| *P.* 'Mrs. Moon'* | Small blue blossoms | 1′ |
| *Sedum* | Small yellow, pink, or white blossoms | ½–12″ |
| *Stachys byzantina* (Lamb's ears) | Silver foliage | 8–12″ |
| *Trillium grandiflorum* (Great white trillium) | Large white blossoms | 6–12″ |
| *Viola* | Blue, apricot, yellow, purple, white pansy-shaped blossoms | 6–12″ |

deep blue blossoms, would be quite beautiful, or that the bright blue or purple blooms of *Iris reticulata* with an overplanting of the matlike foliage and tiny brilliant yellow blossoms of *Draba sibirica* would also be quite effective. Look over the list and use your imagination in putting together various combinations.

Following the March and early-April blooming irises and crocuses, and early-blooming daffodils, come the mid- and late-April blooming bulbs. These include:

| BULB | COLOR |
| --- | --- |
| *Anemone blanda* | White, pink, red, or bluish purple |
| *Chionodoxa* (Glory-of-the-snow) | Blue with white eye, pink or white |
| Daffodil | Yellow, gold, white, orange, apricot, or combinations thereof |
| *Fritillaria imperialis* | Red, orange, or yellow |
| *Hyacinthus orientalis* (Dutch hyacinth) | Pink, purple, blue, red, cream, white, yellow, or apricot |
| *Muscari* (Grape hyacinth) | Deep blue, light blue, or white |
| *Puschkinia scilloides* (Striped squill) | Bluish white or white |
| *Scilla siberica* | Bright electric blue |
| *S. tubergeniana* | Pale blue |
| Tulip (Species) | Many colors |

At this point in the season, you have many options for complementing bulb plantings. Refer to the list of perennial plants on the previous page and start planning your April garden.

Following the bloom of *Magnolia stellata* are those of the golden and white forsythias and the early-blooming pink-flowering almond. The blossoms of many April-blooming bulbs look particularly beautiful planted around these early-blooming shrubs.

Some particularly lovely combinations are grape hyacinths planted beneath golden yellow–blooming forsythia. Another, which I spotted in the garden of my neighbor, Mrs. Alice Levian, was utterly inspired. She planted a soft pink stand of Dutch hyacinths beneath a mat of white-flowering arabis.

A drift of electric blue grape hyacinths planted in front of a drift of yellow daffodils is another lovely combination, and when a bank of candytuft lies behind it, it is even more beautiful.

In late April, in most parts of the country, the Triumph tulips bloom. Perhaps the most beautiful is 'Apricot Beauty.' A drift planting of 'Delft Blue' or 'Blue Haze' hyacinths in front of these lovely pastel apricot tulips offers a stunning display.

The month of May is when most tulips come into bloom. Some early-blooming tulips and late-blooming daffodils will still be in bloom, along with some of the later-blooming minor bulbs. These include:

| BULB | COLOR |
| --- | --- |
| *Allium* | Purple, blue, yellow, red pink, or lavender (ornamental onion) |
| *Camassia* (Wild hyacinth) | Blue, cream, or white |
| *Convallaria* (Lily of the valley) | White or pale pink |
| *Eremurus* (Foxtail lily) | White, yellow, orange, cream, rose, pink or peach-pink |
| *Erythronium* | White, yellow, rose-purple, purple, or combinations thereof |

| BULB | COLOR | BULB | COLOR |
|------|-------|------|-------|
| *Fritillaria meleagris* (Guinea hen flower) | Purple and white or white | *Ornithogalum umbellatum* (Star-of-Bethlehem) | White with green stripes |
| *F. michailovskyi* | Bronze and yellow | Tulips | |
| *Hyacinthoides (Scilla) hispanica* | Pink, white, or blue | Cottage | All colors except blue |
| *Ipheion uniflorum* | White | Darwin hybrid | All colors except blue |
| Iris (Dutch) | Yellow, blue, purple, bronze, white, orange, or combinations | Double peony | All colors except blue |
| | | Lily-flowering | All colors except blue |
| | | Parrot | All colors except blue |
| *Leucojum* (Snowflake) | White | Triumph | All colors except blue |

*This spectacular planting of daffodils beneath a flowering crab apple at Keukenhof Gardens in Holland demonstrates just how breathtakingly beautiful a lavish planting of bulbs can be.*

There are many perennials that bloom in May. Here is a list of some that are most suitable for combining with late-spring bulb plantings.

Spring-flowering trees and shrubs are now at their peak and can be used to complement bulb plantings. Think particularly in terms of dogwoods, for their deep pink, light pink, or white blossoms provide a perfect canopy for a large planting of late-blooming tulips. Imagine a lovely white-flowering dogwood with a planting of pink, rose, and pale red Darwin tulips, or a pink-flowering dogwood with a combination of white and pale yellow double peony tulips.

When my white dogwood blooms, I place a thistle bird feeder in its branches. The gold-finches, who relish thistle, decorate the tree with their brilliant yellow plumage. Beneath is a planting of yellow and white tulips. Needless to say, the effect is breathtaking.

Perhaps the most useful of all May-blooming shrubs when planted in tandem with bulbs are azaleas and rhododendrons. Their many shades of pink, red, purple, white, pale yellow, and salmon offer endless color combinations.

Lilacs are also in bloom at this time and combine well with purple, white, yellow, or pink-and-rose tulips, along with deep blue grape hyacinths.

Flowering crab-apple, peach, and apricot trees, as well as apple trees, all sport pink or white

| PERENNIAL | COLOR | HEIGHT |
|---|---|---|
| *Achillea* (Yarrow) | Sulphur yellow, pale yellow, rose, white, or lavender | 2–4' |
| *Ajuga* (Bugleweed) | Deep blue flower spikes | 6" |
| *Anthemis* (Golden marguerite) | Bright yellow daisy-shaped flowers | 2–3' |
| *Aquilegia* (Columbine) | All colors | 1–3' |
| *Arenaria* (Sandwort) | Mats of white blossoms | 6" |
| *Centaurea montana* (Cornflower) | Deep blue | 2–3' |
| *Dianthus* (Pinks) | Many shades of red, pink, salmon, white, or combinations thereof | 3–12" |
| *Dicentra* (Bleeding heart) | Pink or white | 1–2' |
| *Geranium* (Cranesbill) | Blue, pink, magenta, or white | 1–1½' |
| *Geum* | Orange, yellow, crimson, or pink | 1–2' |
| *Heuchera* (Coral bells) | Pink, red, or white | 1–2' |
| Iris (German) | All colors | 2–3' |
| *Myosotis* (Forget-me-not) | Tiny blue blossoms | 1–1½' |
| Peony | Red, pink, yellow, white, or combinations thereof | 2–4' |
| *Phlox divaricata* (Wild phlox) | Blue | 6–15" |
| *P. stolonifera* (Creeping phlox) | Blue, red, pink, or white | 3–6" |
| *P. subulata* (Moss pinks) | Blue, red, pink, or white | 3–6" |
| *Polemonium* (Jacob's ladder) | Blue | 1–2½' |
| *Polygonatum* (Solomon's seal) | Creamy white | ½–4' |
| *Saponaria* (Soapwort) | Pink mats of flowers | 6" |
| *Trollius* (Globeflower) | Bright yellow | 1–1½' |
| *Veronica prostrata* (Speedwell) | Blue mats of flowers | 6" |

Above: *Late-flowering rose-colored 'Queen of Bartignon' tulips bloom simultaneously with white 'Snowflake' dogwood, complementing the snowy blossoms perfectly.* Below: *Pink lily-flowering tulip 'Jacqueline,' coupled with old-fashioned bleeding heart* (Dicentra spectabilis), *sweetly announces spring with its soft coloration.*

blossoms and will also set off a tulip planting. The deep red of hawthorn looks sensational with brilliant red and yellow late-blooming tulips.

# THE MIXED SUMMER BULB GARDEN

There are so very many options open to you when selecting plants to complement a summer bulb planting. Literally hundreds of annuals, perennials, and shrubs bloom during the summer, so it is perhaps better to plan your summer garden using annuals and perennials and then add the summer bulbs that you decide are appropriate for your scheme.

There is, however, a group of summer-blooming bulbs that is shade-loving. With these bulbs—caladiums, tuberous begonias, and colocasia (elephant ears)—you certainly can start with a bulb plan and then amplify it with other shade-loving plants. The bright, colorful foliage of caladiums is set off perfectly by the startling blooms of tuberous begonias. Many caladiums are available in shades of green, pink, and white, and these combine nicely with pink or white or, for that matter, bright red or yellow begonias. A planting of colocasia placed behind the caladiums and begonias makes a lush green backdrop for their colorful foliage and blossoms. Add some pink, white, or red impatiens and a planting of pink or white rubrum lilies and you have an eye-catching shade garden. A border of electric blue lobelia will provide accent, and hostas interplanted will add many levels of green. Rather than selecting a hosta with pale lavender blooms, select the cultivar 'Honeybells,' which is pure white and one of the few scented hostas, possessing a haunting fragrance that is reminiscent of the sweet-smelling tuberose.

Since there are so many options for combining annuals and perennials with summer-blooming bulbs, look over the suggestions for using color in landscape on pages 24–30, then decide what will work best for you. Here are a few tips to help you in your selection.

• Since many summer-flowering bulbs are quite flamboyant in color and blossom size and shape, consider the more delicate-looking annuals, such as cleome and cosmos, and use these in tandem with bulbs, rather than garish zinnias, red salvia, or marigolds.

• Although there are some perennials with a gaudy appearance, most are delicate and subtle, working well with plantings of dahlias, lilies, gladiolas, or tigridias.

• Many gardeners do not find the growth habits and foliage of lilies particularly attractive, so they interplant them with daylilies or hosta. The foliage of these plants obscures the tall, lanky stems of the lilies while they are in bloom as well as the withering stems after the blooms have passed.

• One classic combination you might wish to consider is white Regale lilies with blue delphiniums and pink astilbe. They all usually bloom at the same time and the effect is quite beautiful.

• Consider planting heavily fragrant summer bulbs, such as tuberose and acidanthera, near your patio or porch so you can enjoy their heady fragrance when relaxing in these outdoor areas.

• Be especially careful when selecting dahlias for your garden. Some grow to six or seven feet, sporting blossoms a full foot across. These require staking, and unless you have a very large property, they will be out of scale with your house and garden. Select instead the dwarf or medium-height varieties. Also be aware that

Above: *Blue fescue grass softens the formal look of giant alliums* (Allium giganteum). Below: *This planting of red and yellow nonstop-blooming tuberous begonias and green-and-white caladium 'Candidum' is set against a backdrop of 'Honeybell' hosta, pale blue globe thistle* (Echinops), *rose-purple coneflower* (Echinacea), *with electric blue annual lobelia and white* Oxalis regnelli *in the foreground.*

many dahlias are very gaudy in appearance. Don't be tempted by brilliantly colored cultivars. They may look sensational in a mail-order catalogue, but they will probably overwhelm your garden.

• Because of their very stiff appearance, gladiolas are especially difficult to use in a combined perennial/annual/summer bulb garden. However, if you plant them in clumps, here and there at the rear of your bed and border, and use subtle colors, they can be effective.

• *Speciosum* and Aurelian hybrid lilies are useful in adding color to a shrub border of broad-leaved evergreens, such as rhododendrons and azaleas. After the shrubs' glorious spring bloom has passed, the lilies will add color throughout the summer.

*In this old-fashioned country garden, pink-and-white annual cleome blends nicely with the native American turk's-cap lily* (Lilium superbum). *For contrast, sulphur yellow 'Coronation Gold' yarrow* (Achillea) *is used sparingly. The deep red hollyhocks planted in front of the weathered fence are not yet in full flower.*

*White-and-green 'Candidum' caladiums perfectly complement the lacy ferns planted in this shade garden.*

• Oxalis is an ideal summer ground cover in shaded areas.

• Agapanthus is a perfect summer-blooming bulb to use in a container on the patio or terrace. The soft blue or white adds a cool touch to the summer patio landscape.

## THE MIXED FALL BULB GARDEN

Since the fall-blooming bulbs are few, there is little reason to plan a fall-blooming bulb garden. Rather, use them as accents in an already planned, established garden. The various autumn crocuses and colchicums are effective when planted along paths to add a dash of color. Late-blooming dahlias blend nicely with chrysanthemums in complementary colors and late-blooming acidantheras, with their white, star-shaped blossoms, can also add an accent to a chrysanthemum planting.

# *Chapter Four*

# BLOOMING BULBS
# FOR SPRING

Beyond a few early blooming shrubs, the first color in the garden each year is that of the glorious bulbs of late winter and early spring. Oh, yes, we're all familiar with the "major" bulbs of spring: the tulips, hyacinths, crocuses, and daffodils, and indeed the spectacle they present each year is a sure sign that winter is over and spring is under way.

However, there are scores of little-known, very inexpensive bulbs, almost all totally maintenance-free and pest- and disease-free, with which only the more experienced gardener is familiar. These are known as the "minor" bulbs: electric blue scilla, charming blue-and-white glory-of-the-snow, the early species crocuses, pale blue Lebanon squill, several species of low-growing fritillarias, early-blooming snowdrops and winter aconite, and many others.

Most of the "minor" bulbs put on their show weeks, even months, before the wondrous display of the "major" bulbs. Give them serious consideration, as there is nothing quite as uplifting to the spirits during the dreary days of late February, March, and early April as having clusters of color in your garden or, better yet, at your dooryard to view as you come and go in the cold snow or rain of late winter.

## *Allium*
### FLOWERING ONION, FLOWERING GARLIC

These bulbs belong to the same family as onions, chives, garlic, shallots, and leeks. Easily grown, there are many cultivars suitable for the garden. Some adapt well to bed and border plantings, others to rockeries.

*Type of bulb:* True bulb.
*Color:* Purple, blue, yellow, pink, red, or lavender.
*Description:* Large, round flower heads or small,

flat flower heads, depending on species, held on erect stems over onionlike foliage.

*Height:* 6 inches to 5 feet, depending on species.

*USDA zones:* 4 to 11.

*Soil:* Well drained, sandy, enriched with sphagnum peat moss and well-rotted compost or manure.

*Light:* Prefers full sun.

*Moisture:* Keep well watered during growing season; do not water once foliage begins to yellow.

*Time to plant:* Fall.

*Planting depth:* Two to three times the diameter of the bulb. For example, giant allium bulbs are 3 to 4 inches in diameter; plant these 6 to 10 inches deep. Smaller bulbs can be planted 2 to 3 inches deep.

*Spacing:* Small bulbs can be planted 4 to 6 inches apart; larger bulbs, 12 to 18 inches apart.

*Care during growing season:* Do not remove foliage until completely withered and brown.

Allium aflatunense, *with its lilac-purple flower heads and chivelike foliage, adds an interesting touch of texture to this rockery.*

## Recommended Alliums

| SPECIES | COLOR | BLOOM TIME | HEIGHT |
| --- | --- | --- | --- |
| A. aflatunense | Lavender | Mid-spring | 3–5' |
| A. atropurpureum | Deep purple | Midsummer | 2½' |
| A. caeruleum | Sky blue | Midsummer | 1½' |
| A. christophii (Star of Persia) | Deep purple | Late spring | 1½' |
| A. elatum | Violet | Late spring | 4–5' |
| A. giganteum (Giant allium) | Lavender | Late spring | 5–6' |
| A. moly* | Yellow | Late spring | 9–18" |
| A. neapolitanum (Flowering onion)* | White | Late spring | 1' |
| A. rosenbachianum | Violet | Midsummer | 4–5' |
| A. roseum* | Rose | Late spring | 12–14" |
| A. sphaerocephalon | Deep purple | Midsummer | 2½' |

*Good for naturalizing.

*Here, the stately stalks of giant alliums* (Allium giganteum) *are set off by a companion planting of sweet-scented lavender.*

Scratch any kind of garden fertilizer into the soil around the plants in spring after shoots emerge.

*Bloom time:* Late spring through summer and into fall, depending on the species.

*Length of bloom:* 1 month.

*Propagation:* After the foliage yellows, dig up and remove any small bulbs that have formed around larger ones. Plant these in late summer or fall. Some species develop bulbs on the tops of faded flowers. Simply remove and plant in late summer or fall.

*Rodent-proof:* Yes.

*Forcing:* No.

*Naturalizing:* Yes, depending on species.

*Endangered species in the wild:* No.

## Anemone blanda
GREEK ANEMONE

These lovely flowers brighten any landscape in the early days of spring. The white variety is particularly effective when overplanted with 'Red Riding Hood' tulips. You should soak the rhizomes in room-temperature water for forty-eight hours before planting.

*Type of bulb:* Rhizome.

*Color:* Bluish purple, pink, red, or white.

*Description:* Daisylike blossoms on low-growing medium green leafy foliage.

*Height:* 4 to 6 inches.

*USDA zones:* 6 to 11.

*Soil:* Well drained, ordinary, fortified with sphagnum peat moss and well-rotted compost or manure.

*Light:* Full sun or partial shade.

*Moisture:* No special moisture requirements. Since rhizomes are dormant during the summer months, it is not necessary to water during periods of drought.

*Time to plant:* Fall.

*Planting depth:* 1 to 2 inches.

*Spacing:* 4 to 6 inches apart.

*Care during growing season:* Do not remove foliage until completely withered and brown. Do not fertilize after initial planting.

*Bloom time:* Early to mid-spring.

*Length of bloom:* 2 to 4 weeks.

*Propagation:* If after a few years vigor and bloom quality have declined, then after the foliage has withered in midsummer, dig tubers and

*This blanket of charming daisy-shaped* Anemone blanda *is punctuated by several 'Red Riding Hood' Greigii tulips.*

divide by cutting with a sharp knife, being sure that each division has at least one eye. Dust cuts with a fungicide powder, available at garden centers and nurseries, let dry in a dry, warm, shady place for two days, and replant. However, since tubers arevery inexpensive, it is probably easier to dig up the old, buy new ones, and replant in the fall.

*Rodent-proof:* No.

*Forcing:* No.

*Naturalizing:* Yes.

*Endangered species in the wild:* Yes. As of 1990, *Anemone blanda*, which have been harvested in the wild and are offered by Netherlands bulb growers, will bear labels stating "Bulbs from Wild Source." Those unmarked are grown from cultivated stock. As of 1992, labels will state place of origin and will be marked "Bulbs Grown from Cultivated Stock" or "Bulbs from Wild Source." See page 143 for more information.

## *Bulbocodium vernum*
### SPRING MEADOW SAFFRON

Although far from spectacular, these delicate little plants add a charming touch of late-winter, early-spring color to a rock garden or edge of a border.

*Type of bulb:* Corm.

*Color:* Pink.

*Description:* 1- to 2-inch, lily-shaped blossoms, followed by medium green spearlike foliage.

*Height:* Blossoms—4 inches; foliage—5 to 6 inches.

*USDA zones:* 3 to 11.

*Soil:* Well drained, ordinary, fortified with sphagnum peat moss and well-rotted compost or manure.

*Light:* Full sun or light shade.

*Moisture:* Water only if spring season is dry. Plant is dormant in summer and requires no special watering.

*Time to plant:* Early fall.

*Planting depth:* 3 inches.

*Spacing:* 4 inches apart.

*Care during growing season:* Do not remove foliage until completely withered and brown. It is not necessary to fertilize after initial planting.

*Bloom time:* Late winter/early spring.

*Length of bloom:* Two weeks.

*Propagation:* Dig up every 2 to 4 years, after foliage has died down in midsummer. Remove the small corms growing around the large ones; store the small corms in a dry, shady place and plant in early fall.

*Rodent-proof:* No.

*Forcing:* No.

*Naturalizing:* Yes, works well in meadows and under trees.

*Endangered species in the wild:* No.

*The early-blooming purple blossoms of* Bulbocodium vernum *come up year in and year out with little, if any, care.*

*Moisture:* Thrives in normal to wet ground. Keep well watered during growing season. Since plants go dormant during summer, no special care is needed at that time.

*Time to plant:* Fall.

*Planting depth:* 3 to 4 inches.

*Spacing:* 3 to 6 inches apart.

*Care during growing season:* Do not remove foliage until completely withered and brown. It is not necessary to fertilize after initial planting.

*Bloom time:* Late spring.

*Length of bloom:* 2 weeks.

*Propagation:* If and when bloom and vigor diminish, dig up after foliage withers and divide; replant in the fall.

*Rodent-proof:* Yes.

*Forcing:* No.

*Naturalizing:* Yes.

*Endangered species in the wild:* No.

## Camassia
CAMASS, QUAMASH, WILD HYACINTH

A native plant that American Indians discovered was poisonous when raw but edible after cooking. These naturalize nicely in wooded areas with dappled shade. Far from spectacular, camasses are grown for their wildflower charm.

*Type of bulb:* True bulb.

*Color:* Blue, cream, or white.

*Description:* Spikes of 1-inch star-shaped blossoms held on stalks over long, thin, grasslike leaves.

*Height:* 1 to 4 feet, depending on species.

*USDA zones:* 3 to 11.

*Soil:* Well drained, ordinary, fortified with sphagnum peat moss and well-rotted compost or manure.

*Light:* Full sun or partial shade.

## Chionodoxa
GLORY-OF-THE-SNOW

These charming early-blooming bulbs should be planted more widely. Once planted, they require absolutely no care and readily multiply into substantial clumps. Despite the fact that the stems are short, they are suitable for early spring cutflower arrangements.

*Type of bulb:* True bulb.

*Color:* Medium blue with white eye, pink, or white.

*Description:* 8 to 10 1-inch star-shaped blooms held on stems over low-growing, medium green spearlike foliage.

*Height:* 4 to 5 inches.

*USDA zones:* 3 to 11.

*Soil:* Well drained, ordinary. Do not enrich the

*Sparkling sky-blue-and-white glory-of-the-snow* (Chionodoxa) *has been naturalized under this birch and contrasts nicely with the white bark of the tree.*

soil or add fertilizer.

*Light:* Full sun or partial shade.

*Moisture:* Average.

*Time to plant:* Fall.

*Planting depth:* 3 inches.

*Spacing:* 1 to 3 inches apart.

*Care during growing season:* If you do not wish chionodoxa to throw seedlings, remove the blossoms when spent. Allow the foliage to ripen and wither before removing it. It is not necessary to fertilize.

*Bloom time:* Early spring.

*Length of bloom:* 2 to 4 weeks.

*Propagation:* It is best to leave bulbs undisturbed—since they are so inexpensive, it is hardly worth dividing them. However, if you do decide to divide them, dig them up after they bloom, remove the small bulbs that have developed around the larger ones, and replant. Seeds from the blossoms will self-sow and spread throughout the garden. This plant is not invasive.

*Rodent-proof:* No.

*Forcing:* No.

*Naturalizing:* Yes.

*Endangered species in the wild:* No.

## Convallaria

LILY OF THE VALLEY

These old-fashioned favorites are very easily grown, and beyond their charm, the foliage serves as an excellent, noninvasive ground cover in shady areas.

*Type of bulb:* Rhizome.
*Color:* White or pink.
*Description:* Bell-shaped blossoms, with a lovely fragrance, on stems over broad, medium green foliage.
*Height:* 8 inches.
*USDA zones:* 3 to 7. Not suitable for warmer climates.
*Soil:* Prefers slightly acid soil, so add sphagnum peat moss and a handful of Miracid to planting site.
*Light:* Partial shade.
*Moisture:* Prefers moist conditions.
*Time to plant:* Fall.
*Planting depth:* 1 inch.
*Spacing:* 3 to 4 inches apart.
*Care during growing season:* Mulch each fall with compost or sphagnum peat moss. It is not necessary to fertilize after initial planting.
*Bloom time:* Late spring.
*Length of bloom:* 2 weeks.
*Propagation:* Divide pips in fall when foliage starts to yellow.
*Rodent-proof:* Yes.
*Forcing:* Yes, but use only prechilled, potted rhizomes available at garden centers, nurseries, and through some mail-order sources.
*Naturalizing:* Yes, particularly under deciduous trees.
*Endangered species in the wild:* No.

## Crocus (Dutch)

Along with tulips and daffodils, the most popular spring bulbs are Dutch crocus. An early-spring garden without substantial plantings of Dutch crocus sporting their brilliant gold, deep purple, lilac, or white blossoms is surely like a field without flowers. They are quite inexpensive, and no matter how many you plant, it is never too much.

*Type of bulb:* Corm.
*Color:* Deep purple, white, yellow, lilac, or striped pale or deep lilac.
*Description:* 1- to 2-inch goblet-shaped blossoms on stems over medium green-and-white grasslike foliage.
*Height:* 2 to 6 inches.
*USDA zones:* 3 to 11.
*Soil:* Well drained, ordinary, fortified with sphagnum peat moss and well-rotted compost or manure.
*Light:* Full sun or partial shade.
*Moisture:* Water only if spring season is dry. Plant is dormant in summer.
*Time to plant:* As early in fall as possible.
*Planting depth:* 2 to 4 inches.
*Spacing:* 2 to 6 inches apart.
*Care during growing season:* Do not remove foliage until completely withered and brown. Each spring, when shoots emerge, scratch in one tablespoon of 9-9-6 fertilizer per square foot of planting area.
*Bloom time:* Late winter/early spring.
*Length of bloom:* 3 weeks.
*Propagation:* In late spring, after foliage has withered and browned, dig up corms, separate, and replant.
*Rodent-proof:* No.
*Forcing:* Yes, some cultivars. See page 136.
*Naturalizing:* Yes.
*Endangered species in the wild:* No.

## Recommended Dutch Crocus

| CULTIVARS | COLOR |
| --- | --- |
| 'Jeanne d'Arc' | White |
| 'Queen of the Blues' | Light blue |
| 'Striped Beauty' | Striped white and pale purple |
| 'The Sultan' | Deep purple |
| 'Yellow Giant' | Deep gold |

liage until completely withered and brown. Each spring, when shoots emerge, scratch in one tablespoon of 9-9-6 fertilizer per square foot of planting area.

*Bloom time:* Late winter to early spring.

*Length of bloom:* 2 weeks.

*Propagation:* It is best to leave corms undisturbed—since they are so inexpensive, it is hardly worth dividing them. However, if you do decide to, dig them up after they bloom, remove the small corms that develop around the larger ones, and replant.

## Crocus (Species)

Less familiar than Dutch crocus are species crocus. These bloom very early, often at the end of January. Although not as spectacular as the Dutch crocus, primarily because they are smaller, if planted in groups of one hundred or more they provide a fine show of color and a needed lift to the winter doldrums.

*Type of bulb:* Corm.

*Color:* Gold, yellow, orange, lemon, light blue, lavender, purple, white, cream, or plum.

*Description:* 1-inch goblet-shaped blossoms on stems over medium green-and-white grasslike foliage

*Height:* 2 to 4 inches.

*USDA zones:* 3 to 11.

*Soil:* Well drained, ordinary, fortified with sphagnum peat moss and well-rotted compost or manure.

*Light:* Full sun or partial shade.

*Moisture:* Water only if spring season is dry. Plant is dormant in summer.

*Time to plant:* Fall.

*Planting depth:* 2 to 4 inches.

*Spacing:* 1 inch apart.

*Care during growing season:* Do not remove fo-

*Here a planting of pale* Crocus chrysanthus *'Blue Pearl' dresses up the early-spring alpine garden.*

*Golden species crocus,* Crocus ancyrensis *'Golden Bunch,' is one of the earliest of all spring bulbs to bloom.*

*Rodent-proof:* No.
*Forcing:* Yes, however, Dutch crocus are better suited to forcing.
*Naturalizing:* Yes.
*Endangered species in the wild:* No.

## *Eranthis*
### WINTER ACONITE

The earliest of all the spring-blooming bulbs, these buttercup yellow blossoms often grow right through the snow and bloom their charming heads off. And, if conditions are right, they will self-sow and naturalize. They are particularly effective in rock gardens.

*Type of bulb:* Tuber.
*Color:* Yellow.

## *Recommended Species Crocus*

| SPECIES OR CULTIVAR | COLOR | HEIGHT |
|---|---|---|
| C. *ancyrensis* 'Golden Bunch' | Deep golden yellow | 4–6″ |
| C. *chrysanthus* 'Advance' | Lemon inside, purple outside | 4–6″ |
| C. *c.* 'Blue Bird' | Deep violet with white margin, white inner petals | 4–6″ |
| C. *c.* 'Blue Pearl' | Delicate blue | 4–6″ |
| C. *c.* 'Canary Bird' | Orange cup with bronze spots | 4–6″ |
| C. *c.* 'Cream Beauty' | Cream white with dark markings | 4–6″ |
| C. *c. fuscotinctus* | Yellow with plum stripes | 4–6″ |
| C. *c.* 'Lady Killer' | Violet-purple edged with white | 4–6″ |
| C. *sieberi* 'Violet Queen' | Amethyst-violet | 4–6″ |
| C. *susianus* ('Cloth of Gold') | Gold tinged with bronze | 4–6″ |
| C. *tommasinianus* 'Ruby Giant' | Pale lavender with darker edges | 4–6″ |
| C. 'White Triumphator' | White with blue veins | 4–6″ |

*Late-winter-blooming, sunny yellow winter aconite* (Eranthis) *is among the first of the spring bulbs to bloom and multiplies readily, becoming more and more spectacular with the passing years.*

*Description:* Small, buttercuplike blossoms set in low-growing, medium green clusters of foliage.

*Height:* 2 to 4 inches.

*USDA zones:* 4 to 9.

*Soil:* Well drained, ordinary, fortified with sphagnum peat moss and well-rotted compost or manure.

*Light:* Full sun or partial shade.

*Moisture:* Water only if spring season is dry. Plant is dormant in summer.

*Time to plant:* As soon as they are available in late summer. Soak in tepid water for 24 hours before planting. The most common cause of failure is late planting; the longer the tubers sit on shelves or in your home, the drier they get, and the less likely they are to grow.

*Planting depth:* 2 to 3 inches.

*Spacing:* 3 to 4 inches apart.

*Care during growing season:* Do not remove foliage until completely withered and brown. It is not necessary to fertilize after the initial planting.

*Bloom time:* Late winter to early spring.

*Length of bloom:* 1 to 2 weeks.

*Propagation:* You can do this even while the plants are in bloom. Dig them up, divide, and replant. Often self-sows.

*Rodent-proof:* No.

*Forcing:* No.

*Naturalizing:* Yes.

*Endangered species in the wild:* Yes. *Eranthis cilicica* and *E. hyemalis* are both gathered in the wild. As of 1990, all eranthis gathered in the wild and offered by Dutch bulb growers will bear labels stating "Bulbs from Wild Source." Those unmarked are grown from cultivated stock. As of 1992, labels will state place of origin and will be marked "Bulbs Grown from Cultivated Stock" or "Bulbs from Wild Source." See page 143 for more information.

## *Eremurus*
FOXTAIL LILY

A handsome plant, nothing short of spectacular; well worth the slight trouble involved in protecting the new shoots in spring.

*Type of bulb:* Tuberous root.

*Color:* White, pink, yellow, orange, cream, rose, or peach-pink.

*Description:* Towering spikes of clustered flowers held on erect stems over straplike foliage.

*Height:* 3 to 9 feet, depending on species.

*USDA zones:* 5 to 9.

*Soil:* Rich, sandy loam, with sphagnum peat moss and well-rotted compost or manure.

*Light:* Full sun.

*Moisture:* Water only if spring season is dry. Plant is dormant in summer.

*Time to plant:* Fall.

*Planting depth:* 6 inches.

*Spacing:* 1½ to 3 feet apart.

*Care during growing season:* Do not remove foliage until completely withered and brown. Mulch each fall with compost and salt hay or wood chips. Remove the mulch early in spring, but until all danger of frost is passed, leave it beside the plants so you can re-cover tender shoots on cold nights.

*Bloom time:* Late spring.

*Length of bloom:* 3 weeks.

*Propagation:* It is best to leave foxtail lilies undisturbed and buy new ones if you want more.

*Rodent-proof:* No.

*Forcing:* No.

*Naturalizing:* Although they can be attractive in a meadow landscape, they do not multiply readily.

*Endangered species in the wild:* No.

## Recommended Eremurus

| SPECIES | COLOR | HEIGHT |
|---|---|---|
| E. himalaicus | White | 6–7′ |
| E. robustus | Pink | 8–9′ |
| E. Shelford Hybrids | Pink, white, yellow, buff, or orange | 4–5′ |

## Erythronium

Most of these are native North American plants, except for the dog-tooth violet (so-called because its blossom is shaped like a dog's tooth), which is native to Europe. Erythroniums are well-suited to woodland gardens, where their delicate blossoms decorate the spring landscape.

*Type of bulb:* Corm.

*Color:* White, yellow, rose-purple, purple, or combinations thereof.

*Description:* 1- to 3-inch-wide lily-shaped blossoms on stalks held over mottled or solid green broad-leaved foliage.

*Height:* 6 inches to 2 feet, depending on species.

*USDA zones:* 3 to 9.

*Soil:* Well drained, ordinary, fortified with sphagnum peat moss and well-rotted compost or manure.

*Light:* Light shade.

*Moisture:* Water only if spring season is dry. Plant is dormant in summer.

*Time to plant:* Summer or fall.

*Planting depth:* 2 to 3 inches.

*Spacing:* 4 to 6 inches apart.

*Care during growing season:* Every 2 or 3 years, apply a top mulch of sphagnum peat moss in the fall.

*Bloom time:* Mid- to late spring.

*Length of bloom:* 2 weeks.

*Propagation:* In summer or fall, dig up and remove the small bulbs that have developed around the larger ones and replant immediately to avoid drying out.

*Rodent-proof:* Yes.

*Forcing:* No.

*Naturalizing:* Yes.

*Endangered species in the wild:* Although they are not on the endangered plant list, it is best not to dig these in the wild; instead, order them from mail-order sources that guarantee they are not collected from the wild.

## Recommended Erythroniums

| SPECIES | COLOR | HEIGHT |
|---|---|---|
| E. albidum (White dog-tooth violet) | White | 1' |
| E. americanum (Trout lily) | Yellow | 1' |
| E. californicum (Fawn lily) | Cream-white | 1' |
| E. dens-canis (Dog-tooth violet) | Rose-purple | 6" |
| E. grandiflorum (Lamb's-tongue fawn lily) | Yellow | 2' |
| E. hendersonii (Henderson fawn lily) | Purple | 1' |
| E. oregonum (Oregon fawn lily) | Cream-white | 1' |
| E. purpurascens (Sierra fawn lily) | Yellow with purple tinge | 1' |
| E. revolutum (Mahogany fawn lily) | Cream with purple tinge | 1' |

## Fritillaria imperialis
CROWN IMPERIAL

The unusual-looking *Fritillaria imperialis* can be added to foundation plantings or borders for mid-spring color. Keep in mind, however, that the blossoms do not smell very pleasant, so they are best grown away from dooryards or house windows.

*Type of bulb:* True bulb.

*Color:* Orange, red ('Rubra'), or yellow ('Lutea Maxima').

*Description:* Clusters of 2-inch-wide blossoms held atop erect stems over clusters of strap-like foliage.

*Height:* 2 to 4 feet.

*USDA zones:* 5 to 11.

*Soil:* Well drained, ordinary, fortified with sphagnum peat moss and well-rotted compost or manure.

*Light:* Partial shade.

*Moisture:* Water only if spring season is dry. Plant is dormant in summer.

*Time to plant:* Fall.

*Planting depth:* 6 inches.

*Spacing:* 8 inches apart.

*Care during growing season:* Do not remove foliage until completely withered and brown. Each spring, when shoots emerge, scratch in one tablespoon of 9-9-6 fertilizer per square foot of planting area.

*Bloom time:* Mid-spring.

*Length of bloom:* 2 weeks.

*Propagation:* Since plants propagated from small bulbs that have been taken from around larger ones take from 4 to 6 years to flower, it is best to purchase mature bulbs if you want more.

*Rodent-proof:* Yes—all rodents hate the smell of the bulb.

*Forcing:* No.

*Naturalizing:* No.

*Endangered species in the wild:* No.

## Fritillaria meleagris
GUINEA HEN FLOWER

Another spring-blooming bulb that should be more widely grown, these bizarre-looking blossoms add interest to a rock garden and thrive in a woodland landscape.

*Type of bulb:* True bulb.

*Color:* Purple-and-white or white, with checkered pattern.

*Description:* 1½-inch, drooping, bell-shaped blossoms held on thin stalks with grasslike foliage.

*Height:* 12 inches.

*USDA zones:* 5 to 11.

*Soil:* Well drained, ordinary, fortified with sphagnum peat moss and well-rotted compost or manure.

*Light:* Partial shade.

*Moisture:* Water only if spring season is dry. Plant is dormant in summer.

*Time to plant:* Fall.

*Planting depth:* 3 to 4 inches.

*Spacing:* 3 to 4 inches.

*Care during growing season:* Do not remove foliage until completely withered and brown. Each spring, when shoots emerge, scratch in

*The bizarre checkerboard purple patterns and pure white varieties of* Fritillaria meleagris *are always conversation pieces in the garden.*

one tablespoon of 9-9-6 fertilizer per square foot of planting area.

*Bloom time:* Mid-spring.

*Length of bloom:* 1 to 2 weeks.

*Propagation:* It is best to leave bulbs undisturbed; they are so inexpensive, it is hardly worth dividing them. However, if you do decide to, dig them up after they bloom, remove the small bulbs that have developed around the larger ones, and replant.

*Rodent-proof:* Yes—all rodents hate the smell of the bulb.

*Forcing:* No.

*Naturalizing:* Will multiply somewhat in a woodland naturalized landscape.

*Endangered species in the wild:* No.

## *Fritillaria michailovskyi*
MICHAEL'S FLOWER

This charming fritillaria has only recently become available through mail-order nurseries in the United States and Canada. I found them a delightful addition to my rock garden.

*Type of bulb:* True bulb.

*Color:* Bronze-maroon with broad yellow edges.

*Description:* 2 or 3 1½-inch bell-shaped blossoms held on drooping stems over broad, straplike foliage.

*Height:* 8 to 12 inches.

*USDA zones:* 5 to 11.

*Soil:* Well drained, ordinary, fortified with sphagnum peat moss and well-rotted compost or manure.

*Light:* Partial shade.

*Moisture:* Water only if spring season is dry. Plant is dormant in summer.

*Time to plant:* Fall.

*Planting depth:* 3 to 4 inches.

*The unusual colorations of the only recently available* Fritillaria michailovskyi, *with their bell-shaped blooms, bring an exotic touch to the early-spring rockery.*

*Spacing:* 3 to 4 inches apart.

*Care during growing season:* Do not remove foliage until completely withered and brown. Each spring, when shoots emerge, scratch in one tablespoon of 9-9-6 fertilizer per square foot of planting area.

*Bloom time:* Mid-spring.

*Length of bloom:* 1 to 2 weeks.

*Propagation:* It is best to leave bulbs undisturbed; however, if you do decide to propagate more, dig them up after they bloom, remove the small bulbs that have developed around the larger ones, and replant.

*Rodent-proof:* Yes—all rodents hate the smell of the bulb.

*Forcing:* No.

*Naturalizing:* Will multiply somewhat in a woodland naturalized landscape.

*Endangered species in the wild:* No.

## Galanthus
SNOWDROP

Along with winter aconite, snowdrops are the earliest blooming of all the spring bulbs. Once they are planted, leave them where they are; each year the bloom display will become lusher and more dramatic.

*Type of bulb:* True bulb.

*Color:* Translucent white.

*Description:* ½-inch bell-shaped blossoms held on stalks over slender, medium green foliage.

*Height:* 3 to 8 inches, depending on species.

*USDA zones:* 3 to 9.

*Soil:* Well drained, ordinary, fortified with sphagnum peat moss and well-rotted compost or manure.

*Light:* Full sun or partial shade.

*Moisture:* Water only if spring season is dry. Plant is dormant in summer.

*Time to plant:* Early fall.

*Planting depth:* 2 to 4 inches.

*Spacing:* 2 to 3 inches apart.

*Care during growing season:* Do not remove foliage until completely withered and brown. It is not necessary to fertilize after the original planting.

*Bloom time:* Late winter/early spring.

*Length of bloom:* 3 to 4 weeks.

*The classic* Galanthus nivalis *is the first of the spring bulbs to bloom, often pushing its head right up through the snow-covered landscape.*

*Propagation:* It is best to leave bulbs undisturbed; they are so inexpensive, it is hardly worth dividing them. However, if you do decide to, dig them up after they bloom, remove the small bulbs that have developed around the larger ones, and replant.

*Rodent-proof:* Yes.

*Forcing:* No.

*Naturalizing:* Yes.

*Endangered species in the wild:* G. nivalis (common snowdrop) is not harvested in the wild. All others are. As of 1990, all galanthus that are harvested in the wild and offered by Dutch bulb growers will bear labels stating "Bulbs from Wild Source." Those unmarked are grown from cultivated stock. As of 1992, labels will state place of origin and will be marked "Bulbs Grown from Cultivated Stock" or "Bulbs from Wild Source." See page 143 for more information.

## Recommended Galanthus

| SPECIES | COLOR | HEIGHT |
| --- | --- | --- |
| G. *elwesii* (Giant snowdrop) | White | 6–9″ |
| G. *nivalis* 'Flore Pleno' | White | 4–6″ |
| G. *n.* 'S. Arnott' | White | 6–10″ |

## Hyacinthoides (Scilla) hispanica
SPANISH BLUEBELL

These semi-tall-growing bulbs should be planted more widely. They are ideal for naturalizing in wooded areas. I prefer the blue and white varieties rather than the pink, which has a washed-out look when in bloom.

*Type of bulb:* True bulb.

*Color:* Blue, white, or pink.

*Description:* Spiky clusters of 1-inch-wide bell-shaped blossoms held on stalks over medium green straplike foliage.

*Height:* 1 foot.

*USDA zones:* 4 to 11.

*Soil:* Ordinary.

*Light:* Full sun or partial shade.

*Moisture:* Water only if spring season is dry. Plant is dormant in summer.

*Time to plant:* Fall.

*Planting depth:* 3 to 4 inches.

*Spacing:* 6 to 8 inches apart.

*Care during growing season:* Do not remove foliage until completely withered and brown. It is not necessary to fertilize after the original planting.

*Bloom time:* Late spring.

*Length of bloom:* 2 weeks.

*Propagation:* Bulbs multiply rapidly, so dig up after flowering, divide, and replant immedi-

Hyacinthoides (Scilla) hispanica, *or Spanish blue-bells, is among the last of the spring-blooming bulbs to flower and combines well with the late-blooming tulips.*

ately or store over the summer in a cool, airy place and plant in fall.
*Rodent-proof:* No.
*Forcing:* No.
*Naturalizing:* Yes.
*Endangered species in the wild:* No.

## *Hyacinthus orientalis*

Familiar to all, Dutch hyacinths are easily grown in the garden. However, their stiff appearance makes them difficult to use effectively in most landscapes. After their first year of bloom, though, the stalks of flowerlets loosen up substantially, taking on a softer, more informal look. They bear a lovely scent both in the garden and as cut flowers.

*Type of bulb:* True bulb.
*Color:* Blue, purple, red, pink, yellow, cream, white, or apricot.
*Description:* Columnar spikes of flowerlets held over jade green straplike foliage.
*Height:* 8 to 12 inches.
*USDA zones:* 4 to 11.
*Soil:* Well drained, ordinary, fortified with sphagnum peat moss and well-rotted compost or manure.
*Light:* Full sun or partial shade.
*Moisture:* Water only if spring season is dry. Plant is dormant in summer.
*Time to plant:* Early fall.
*Planting depth:* 5 to 6 inches.
*Spacing:* 5 inches apart.
*Care during growing season:* Do not remove foliage until completely withered and brown. Each spring, when shoots emerge, scratch in one tablespoon of 9-9-6 fertilizer per square foot of planting area.
*Bloom time:* Early to mid-spring.
*Length of bloom:* 3 weeks.
*Propagation:* It is best to purchase new bulbs rather than to try to propagate from existing stock.
*Rodent-proof:* Yes.
*Forcing:* Yes, some cultivars. See page 136.
*Naturalizing:* No.
*Endangered species in the wild:* No.

## Recommended Hyacinths

| CULTIVAR | COLOR |
| --- | --- |
| 'Marconi' | Pink |
| 'Lady Derby' | Rosy pink |
| 'Pink Pearl' | Rosy pink |
| 'Queen of the Pinks' | Rich pink |
| 'Jan Bos' | Scarlet-red |
| 'City of Haarlem' | Bright yellow |
| 'Gypsy Queen' | Soft orange-peach |
| 'Carnegie' | Pure white |
| 'L' Innocence' | Pure white |
| 'White Pearl' | Pure white |
| 'Blue Haze' | Light blue |
| 'Perle Brilliante' | Light blue |
| 'Blue Giant' | Medium blue |
| 'Blue Jacket' | Bright blue |
| 'Delft Blue' | Dark blue |
| 'King of the Blues' | Dark blue |

*A spectacular planting of deep red 'Jan Bos' hyacinths, installed in a large tub planter, adds a zesty accent to an otherwise colorless part of a landscape.*

## Ipheion uniflorum
SPRING STARFLOWER

This nearly indestructible plant blooms freely in sun or shade, but be careful where you plant it—it can be invasive.

*Type of bulb:* True bulb.
*Color:* White.
*Description:* 1-inch-wide star-shaped blossoms that smell of a hint of mint held on stalks over grassy leaves.
*Height:* 6 inches.
*USDA zones:* 6 to 11.
*Soil:* Well drained, ordinary. Do not enrich soil or add fertilizer, compost, or manure.
*Light:* Full sun or partial shade.
*Moisture:* Water only if spring season is dry.

Plant is dormant in summer.
*Time to plant:* Late summer/early fall.
*Planting depth:* 3 inches.
*Spacing:* 6 inches apart.
*Care during growing season:* Do not remove foliage until completely withered and brown. It is not necessary to fertilize.
*Bloom time:* Late spring.
*Length of bloom:* 2 weeks.
*Propagation:* It is best to leave bulbs undisturbed; since they multiply so readily, it is hardly worth dividing them. However, if you do decide to, dig them up after they bloom, remove the small bulbs that have developed around the larger ones, and replant.
*Rodent-proof:* Yes.
*Forcing:* No.

*Naturalizing:* Yes, multiplying to the point that they may become a nuisance.
*Endangered species in the wild:* No.

## *Iris* (Dutch)

These mid-spring–blooming hybrids are particularly effective when used as a color and blossom shape in contrast to late-blooming tulips.

*Type of bulb:* True bulb.
*Color:* White, yellow, orange, bronze, blue, purple, or combinations thereof.
*Description:* 3- to 4-inch blossoms on sturdy stalks amid spearlike foliage.
*Height:* 18 to 24 inches.
*USDA zones:* 5 to 10.
*Soil:* Ordinary, with good drainage.
*Light:* Full sun.
*Moisture:* Water copiously from the time the leaves emerge until about a month after the flowers finish. Then withhold water and let foliage die.
*Time to plant:* Fall.
*Planting depth:* 3 to 4 inches.
*Spacing:* 3 to 4 inches apart.
*Care during growing season:* Do not remove foliage until completely withered and brown. Each spring, when shoots emerge, scratch in one tablespoon of 9-9-6 fertilizer per square foot of planting area.
*Bloom time:* Mid-spring.
*Length of bloom:* 1 to 2 weeks.
*Propagation:* Since they are so inexpensive, it is best to purchase bulbs at garden centers or nurseries at fall planting time if you want more.
*Rodent-proof:* No.
*Forcing:* No.
*Naturalizing:* No.
*Endangered species in the wild:* No.

## *Iris danfordiae*

Although they rarely bloom a second year, these charming bright yellow iris are worth the effort of planting every fall. Along with the *Iris reticulata* (see next page), they provide sparkling, late-winter color to any rock garden.

*Type of bulb:* True bulb.
*Color:* Yellow.

*Bright yellow* Iris danfordiae *adds its golden hue to a rockery after the winter aconite (Eranthis) has finished blooming and before the flamboyant display of yellow daffodils.*

*Description:* Iris-shaped blossoms on stems over grasslike foliage.

*Height:* 6 inches.

*USDA zones:* 3 to 8.

*Soil:* Ordinary, with good drainage.

*Light:* Full sun or partial shade.

*Moisture:* Water only if spring season is dry. Plant is dormant in summer.

*Time to plant:* Fall.

*Planting depth:* 3 to 4 inches.

*Spacing:* 3 to 4 inches apart.

*Care during growing season:* Do not remove foliage until completely withered and brown. Each spring, when shoots emerge, scratch in one tablespoon of 9-9-6 fertilizer per square foot of planting area.

*Bloom time:* Late winter/early spring.

*Length of bloom:* 1 to 2 weeks.

*Propagation:* Not practical; bulbs rarely thrive more than two seasons. Replace with new ones.

*Rodent-proof:* Yes.

*Forcing:* Yes. See page 136.

*Naturalizing:* No.

*Endangered species in the wild:* No.

The delicate blossoms of Iris reticulata *exude a delicate, sweet fragrance and can be picked and included in mini–flower arrangements indoors.*

## Iris reticulata

These very-early-blooming, low-growing iris bloom as early as late February in my rock garden. Coupled with *Iris danfordiae*'s bright yellow blossoms, they certainly give a substantial lift to the late winter doldrums.

*Type of bulb:* True bulb.

*Color:* Light blue or lavender and purple.

*Description:* Iris-shaped blossoms on stems held over grasslike foliage.

*Height:* 6 inches.

*USDA zones:* 3 to 8.

*Soil:* Ordinary, with good drainage.

*Light:* Full sun or partial shade.

*Moisture:* Water only if spring season is dry. Plant is dormant in summer.

*Time to plant:* Fall.

*Planting depth:* 3 to 4 inches.

*Spacing:* 3 to 4 inches apart.

*Care during growing season:* Do not remove foliage until completely withered and brown. Each spring, when shoots emerge, scratch in one tablespoon of 9-9-6 fertilizer per square foot of planting area.

*Bloom time:* Late winter/early spring.

*Length of bloom:* 1 to 2 weeks.

*Propagation:* In the unlikely event that bulbs multiply to the point that flowering diminishes, then, in midsummer, when foliage has completely dried, dig up the bulb clump, separate, and replant immediately.

*Rodent-proof:* Yes.

*Forcing:* Yes. See page 136.

*Naturalizing:* No.

*Endangered species in the wild:* No.

## *Leucojum*
### SNOWFLAKE

Similar to the early-blooming galanthus, these little jewels sport larger blossoms and grow taller. They offer a lingering look at spring in the rockery, where they are particularly effective.

*Type of bulb:* True bulb.

*Color:* White.

*Description:* 1-inch bell-shaped blossoms held on stems over slender, medium green foliage.

*Height:* 9 inches.

*USDA zones:* 4 to 11.

*Soil:* Well drained, ordinary, fortified with sphagnum peat moss and well-rotted compost or manure.

*Light:* Full sun or partial shade.

*Moisture:* Water only if spring season is dry. Plant is dormant in summer.

*Time to plant:* Early fall.

*Planting depth:* 3 to 4 inches.

*Spacing:* 4 inches apart.

*Care during growing season:* Do not remove foliage until completely withered and brown. It is not necessary to fertilize after the initial planting.

*Bloom time:* Late spring.

*Although similar in appearance to snowdrops (Galanthus),* the bell-shaped blossoms of snowflakes (Leucojum aestivum) *appear late in the spring.*

*Length of bloom:* 2 weeks.

*Propagation:* It is best to leave bulbs undisturbed; they are so inexpensive, it is hardly worth dividing them. However, if you do decide to, dig them up after they bloom, remove the small bulbs that have developed around the larger ones, and replant.

*Rodent-proof:* No.

*Forcing:* No.

*Naturalizing:* Yes.

*Endangered species in the wild:* Yes. As of 1990, all leucojum that are harvested in the wild and offered by Dutch bulb growers will bear labels stating "Bulbs from Wild Source." Those unmarked are grown from propagated stock. As of 1992, labels will state place of origin and will be marked "Bulbs Grown from Cultivated Stock" or "Bulbs from Wild Source." See page 143 for more information.

## Muscari
### GRAPE HYACINTH

When in bloom, most varieties of these charming bulbs resemble bunches of grapes hung upside down. They perfume the surrounding air with lovely, subtle, sweet fragrance and are well suited to rock gardens.

*Type of bulb:* True bulb.
*Color:* Bright blue, pale blue, or white.
*Description:* Clusters of flowers held on stems over sprawling, straplike foliage.
*Height:* 4 to 12 inches, depending on species.
*USDA zones:* 2 to 11.
*Soil:* Well drained, ordinary, fortified with sphagnum peat moss and well-rotted compost or manure.
*Light:* Full sun or partial shade.
*Moisture:* Water only if spring season is dry. Plant is dormant in summer.
*Time to plant:* Fall.
*Planting depth:* 3 inches.
*Spacing:* 3 inches apart.
*Care during growing season:* Allow the foliage to ripen and wither before removing it. It will not be necessary to fertilize after the original planting.
*Bloom time:* Mid-spring.
*Length of bloom:* 3 weeks.

Muscari armeniacum *(grape hyacinth) offer their electric blue color to accent the yellow and whites of other spring-blooming bulbs.*

*Propagation:* It is best to leave bulbs undisturbed; since they are so inexpensive, it is hardly worth dividing them. However, if you do decide to, dig them up after they bloom, remove the small bulbs that have developed around the larger ones, and replant.
*Rodent-proof:* No.
*Forcing:* Yes, but only *M. armeniacum.* See page 136.
*Naturalizing:* Yes.
*Endangered species in the wild:* No.

## Recommended Muscari

| SPECIES | COLOR | HEIGHT |
|---|---|---|
| *M. armeniacum* | Blue clusters | 4–8″ |
| *M. a.* 'Album' | White clusters | 4–8″ |
| *M. a.* 'Blue Spike' | Double blue clusters | 10–12″ |
| *M. plumosum* | Featherlike plumes | 6–8″ |
| (Feather hyacinth) | | |

Muscari plumosum *sports featherlike plumed blossoms, offering a softer look than its more common cousin,* M. armeniacum.

## Narcissus
### DAFFODIL

Daffodils are probably the most universally grown and loved of all the spring-flowering bulbs for practical as well as aesthetic reasons: They are not only pest- and disease-free but also rodent-proof. Most varieties perform well over a period of five, ten, even fifteen to twenty years—though some do not. After the first three years, some varieties form thick clumps of foliage but steadily produce fewer flowers. In some instances, the bulbs die out completely. In 1972, at the Planting Fields Arboretum on Long Island, New York, a daffodil planting trial was begun in which two hundred different varieties of daffodils, representing twenty classifications, were planted in groups of six bulbs each. They were left undisturbed, and the number of flowers produced was tabulated each year. After ten years, some varieties were strong and still flowering to perfection. Others had fewer flowers, while still others had disappeared completely. The varieties that consistently produced a lavish display were:

- 'Arctic Gold'
- 'Binkie'
- 'Broughshane'
- 'Cantabile'
- 'Carlton'
- 'Cherie'
- 'Dove Wings'
- 'Duke of Windsor'
- 'February Gold'
- 'Flower Record'
- 'Ice Follies'
- 'March Sunshine'
- 'Mrs. R. O. Backhouse'
- 'Red Rascal'
- 'Spellbinder'
- 'Sun Chariot'

*Perhaps no other bulb is so effective as the daffodil when a naturalized effect is desired. Carefree and disease and pest resistant, once planted they will bloom for decades.*

- 'Sweetness'
- 'Thalia'
- 'Trevithian'
- 'Winifred van Graven'

The Netherlands Bulb Industry also conducted a series of four-year trials at the North Carolina State University Arboretum. Again, some varieties of daffodils performed better than others. Here is a list of those that produced the best displays year after year:

- 'Barrett Browning'

- 'Brighton'
- 'Carbineer'
- 'Estella de Mol'
- 'February Gold'
- 'Flower Record'
- 'Fortune'
- 'Gigantic Star'
- 'Ice Follies'
- 'Jumblie'
- 'Salome'
- 'Sugarbush'
- 'Tahiti'
- 'Thalia'

- 'Tresamble'
- 'Trevithian'

*Type of bulb:* True bulb.
*Color:* White, yellow, gold, orange, or apricot.
*Description:* There are eleven basic types of narcissus according to a system established by the Royal Horticultural Society of Great Britain and followed by bulb growers throughout the world. Shapes include the familiar trumpet, small-cupped, large-cupped, double, and so forth. All grow on erect stems over medium green swordlike foliage.
*Height:* 3 inches to 2 feet, depending on variety.
*USDA zones:* 4 to 11.
*Soil:* Well drained, ordinary, fortified with sphagnum peat moss and well-rotted compost or manure.
*Light:* Full sun or partial shade.
*Moisture:* Water only if spring season is dry. Plant is dormant in summer.
*Time to plant:* Fall is best; however, I have known people who forgot to plant, installed them in early spring, and they not only survived but bloomed.
*Planting depth:* Three times the diameter of the bulb.
*Spacing:* 6 to 8 inches apart, depending on the size of the bulb.
*Care during growing season:* Do not remove foliage until completely withered and brown. Each spring, when shoots emerge, scratch in one tablespoon of 9-9-6 fertilizer per square foot of planting area.
*Bloom time:* Early to mid-spring, depending on the variety and the location of the planting (those receiving more sun or warmth will bloom earlier).
*Length of bloom:* 2 to 3 weeks.
*Propagation:* If, after a few years, bloom becomes sparse, bulbs have multiplied to the point where they need dividing. After foliage has withered and dried, dig up the bulbs, separate them, and either replant or store for the summer in an airy, shady place and plant in the fall.
*Rodent-proof:* Yes.
*Forcing:* Yes, some cultivars. See page 136.
*Naturalizing:* Yes.
*Endangered species in the wild:* All varieties sold in the United States and Canada are grown from cultivated stock.

## *Narcissus* (Miniature)
MINIATURE DAFFODIL

These mini-sized versions of the standard daffodils add great charm to dooryard gardens, rockeries, and foundation plantings. Still, many gardeners have not yet discovered them. They are very reasonable in price and are a joy to behold in the spring. *Narcissus bulbocodium* is a species miniature, a petite delight at six inches.

*Type of bulb:* True bulb.
*Color:* Yellow, orange, white, or combinations thereof.
*Description:* Trumpet or double blossoms on stalks over medium green spearlike foliage.
*Height:* 6 to 14 inches, depending on variety.
*USDA zones:* 4 to 11.
*Soil:* Well drained, ordinary, fortified with sphagnum peat moss and well-rotted compost or manure.
*Light:* Full sun or partial shade.
*Moisture:* Water only if spring season is dry. Plant is dormant in summer.
*Time to plant:* Fall.
*Planting depth:* 3 to 5 inches.
*Spacing:* 4 to 6 inches apart.
*Care during growing season:* Do not remove foliage until completely withered and brown.

Each spring, when shoots emerge, scratch in one tablespoon of 9-9-6 fertilizer per square foot of planting area.

*Bloom time:* Early to mid-spring.

*Length of bloom:* 3 weeks.

*Propagation:* If, after a few years, bloom becomes sparse, bulbs have multiplied to the point where they need dividing. After the foliage has withered and dried, dig up the bulbs, separate them, and either replant or store for the summer in an airy, shady place and plant in the fall.

*Rodent-proof:* Yes.

*Forcing:* Yes, some cultivars. See pages 136–37.

*Naturalizing:* Yes.

*Endangered species in the wild:* Those sold in the United States and Canada are all propagated from cultivated varieties.

## Recommended Miniature Daffodils

| CULTIVAR | COLOR | HEIGHT |
| --- | --- | --- |
| 'April Tears' | Deep yellow | 6–8" |
| 'Baby Moon' | Buttercup yellow | 9" |
| 'Double Jonquil' | Bright yellow double flowers | 10" |
| 'February Gold' | Bright yellow and lemon | 8" |
| 'Gold Drops' | Yellow and white | 10" |
| 'Hawera' | Creamy yellow | 8" |
| 'Jack Snipe' | White and yellow | 8" |
| 'Liberty Bells' | Clusters of yellow flowers | 8" |
| 'Lintie' | Yellow with orange rim | 9" |
| 'Little Witch' | Deep yellow | 6" |
| 'Peeping Tom' | Golden yellow | 8" |
| 'Pipit' | Sulphur and white | 9" |
| 'Rip van Winkle' | Clear yellow double flowers | 6" |
| 'Suzy' | Yellow and orange | 14" |
| 'Tête-à-Tête' | Yellow | 8" |

*The disarming* Narcissus bulbocodium *(hoop petticoat daffodil) should be planted more widely, for not only does it bring a beguiling touch to a dooryard or rock garden, it can also be cut and combined with other spring-blooming bulbs in indoor arrangements.*

## Ornithogalum umbellatum
### STAR-OF-BETHLEHEM

I found a stand of these growing on the grounds of an old farm nearby, moved them to my property, and planted them under a canopy of maple trees, where they still thrive. While these plants can become invasive, with the shallow roots of the maple absorbing both moisture and nutrients from the soil, they are ideally suited and have not spread aggressively.

*Type of bulb:* True bulb.
*Color:* White with green stripes.
*Description:* Spiky clusters of 1-inch-wide star-shaped fragrant blossoms held on stalks over medium green straplike foliage.
*Height:* 1 to 2 feet.
*USDA zones:* 4 to 11.
*Soil:* Ordinary.
*Light:* Full sun or partial shade.
*Moisture:* Water only if spring season is dry. Plant is dormant in summer.
*Time to plant:* Fall.
*Planting depth:* 2 to 3 inches.
*Spacing:* 6 to 8 inches apart.
*Care during growing season:* Do not remove foliage until completely withered and brown. It is not necessary to fertilize.
*Bloom time:* Late spring.
*Length of bloom:* 2 weeks.
*Propagation:* Dig them up after they bloom, remove the small bulbs that have grown around the larger one, and replant immediately or store over the summer in a cool, airy place and plant in the fall.
*Rodent-proof:* Yes.
*Forcing:* No.
*Naturalizing:* Yes, but beware: They can become invasive.
*Endangered species in the wild:* No.

## Puschkinia scilloides
### STRIPED SQUILL

This is another "minor" bulb that should be more popular than it is. It's ideal for the rock garden or tucked here and there in the front of the border.

*The little-known puschkinia, with its pale blue-and-white blossoms, is another "minor" bulb that is ideal for naturalizing under deciduous trees.*

It will self-sow and naturalize if conditions are favorable.

*Type of bulb:* True bulb.
*Color:* Bluish white or white.
*Description:* Clusters of ½- to 1-inch-wide blossoms held on stalks over straplike leaves.
*Height:* 4 to 8 inches.
*USDA zones:* 3 to 11.
*Soil:* Well drained, ordinary. Do not enrich the soil or add fertilizer, compost, or manure.
*Light:* Full sun or partial shade.
*Moisture:* Water only if spring season is dry. Plant is dormant in summer.
*Time to plant:* Fall.
*Planting depth:* 2 to 3 inches.
*Spacing:* 2 to 3 inches apart.
*Care during growing season:* If you do not wish puschkinia to throw seedlings, remove its

blossoms when they are spent. Allow the foliage to ripen and wither before removing it. It is not necessary to fertilize.

*Bloom time:* Early spring.

*Length of bloom:* 3 to 4 weeks.

*Propagation:* It is best to leave bulbs undisturbed; they are so inexpensive, it is hardly worth dividing them. However, if you do decide to, dig them up after they bloom, remove the small bulbs that have developed around the larger ones, and replant.

*Rodent-proof:* No.

*Forcing:* No.

*Naturalizing:* Yes.

*Endangered species in the wild:* No.

## *Scilla siberica* and *S. tubergeniana*

The sensationally beautiful electric blue blossoms of *Scilla siberica*, or Siberian squill, are perhaps my favorite early-spring–blooming bulb. The blossoms of *S. tubergeniana* are pale blue or white and, although charming, do not make the visual impact of the *siberica*.

*Type of bulb:* True bulb.

*Color:* Brilliant blue, pale blue, lilac pink, or white.

*Description:* Bell- or star-shaped blossoms held on stems over straplike leaves.

*Height:* 6 inches.

*USDA zones:* 1 to 8.

*Soil:* Well drained, ordinary. Do not enrich soil.

*Light:* Full sun or partial shade.

*Moisture:* Water only if spring season is dry. Plant is dormant in summer.

*Time to plant:* Fall.

*Planting depth:* 2 to 3 inches.

*Spacing:* 3 to 4 inches apart.

*Among the earliest of flowering bulbs, the startling bright blue of* Scilla siberica *is a welcome sign of spring.*

*Care during growing season:* If you do not wish squill to throw seedlings, remove its blossoms when spent. Allow the foliage to ripen and wither before removing it. It is not necessary to fertilize.

*Bloom time:* Early spring.

*Length of bloom:* 3 to 4 weeks.

*Propagation:* It is best to leave bulbs undisturbed; they are so inexpensive, it is hardly worth dividing them. However, if you do decide to propagate, dig them up after they bloom, remove the small bulbs that have developed around the larger ones, and replant.

*Rodent-proof:* Yes.

*Forcing:* No.

*Naturalizing:* Yes.

*Endangered species in the wild:* No.

## Tulipa

In Holland, and indeed throughout Europe, most gardeners treat tulips as annuals—that is, they plant them in the fall and then, after bloom, dig them up and throw them away. They do this because they know that most tulips produce less and less bloom with each passing year. Here in America, however, we tend to think in terms of permanent, perennial plantings, so we plant tulips and then, several years down the line, wonder why they no longer produce spectacular blooms. The reason is that tulip bulbs divide into small bulbs each year, and if the planting is not fertilized and the soil structure and climate are not ideal, they deplete. Even under optimal conditions the blooms usually become smaller and smaller, eventually disappearing.

For that reason, most tulips cannot be counted on to enhance your garden scheme after a year or two. Some varieties are more prone to "perennialize" than others—that is, to provide a continuing display year after year—but they must be fertilized properly to achieve this effect. Beyond this, conditions vary to such an extent from area to area, from garden to garden, and even within an individual garden, that you cannot count on true perennialization of tulips. However, tulips are so beautiful that it is certainly worth experimenting with those varieties that do tend to perennialize.

There are many types of tulips available. Species tulips, most of which are the earliest to bloom and the closest genetically to the original wild tulips, are classed as Kaufmanniana, Fosteriana or Emperor, and Greigii. All of these tend to perennialize and multiply, providing beautiful displays year after year. Another early-blooming variety, the early-bloom double, does not. Of the other varieties, mid-season Cottage and Triumph, the later-blooming Rembrandt, Parrot, lily-flowering, and Viridiflora, and the hundreds of Darwin cultivars are not prone to perennialize, usually producing less and less bloom each year.

The spectacular Darwin hybrids, a cross between the Fosteriana or Emperor tulip and the Darwin, does tend to perennialize if conditions are favorable. I have a planting of Darwin hybrid 'Golden Apeldoorn,' now in its sixth year, that is more beautiful and carries more blooms than when it was planted.

In addition to those mentioned above, there is a class of wild or near-wild tulips that truly does perennialize. Small in stature and bloom, these tulips usually multiply freely and can be used in rock gardens, dooryard gardens, or anywhere they can be viewed closely. Most are early bloomers and are available from most mail-order sources. See pages 144–45 for a list of them.

So, if you are looking for tulips that perennialize, stick to the low-growing, early-blooming species Kaufmanniana and Greigii; the tall, early-blooming Fosteriana or Emperor tulips; the "wild" tulips; and, for later display, the Darwin hybrids. Of course, the lovely shapes and colors of lily-flowering, Cottage, Darwin, and other tulips may be more than you can resist. If so, by all means plant them, but be prepared for the fact that after a few years they will probably deplete and have to be replaced.

## Tulipa fosteriana
EMPEROR TULIP

These tall, early-blooming tulips that tend to perennialize provide a glimpse of the later spring

*Early-blooming Kaufmanniana tulip 'Shakespeare' resembles a land-loving water lily, brightening any garden during the early spring months.*

glories of tulip bloom. Until recently, only solid colors were available, but each year hybridizers are creating new and interesting varieties that are being offered to gardeners.

*Type of bulb:* True bulb.
*Color:* Red, pink, yellow, white, orange, or combinations thereof.
*Description:* 4-inch turban-shaped blossoms on stems held over medium green or medium-green-and-purple broad-leaved foliage.
*Height:* 16 inches.
*USDA zones:* 3 to 11.
*Soil:* Well drained, ordinary, fortified with sphagnum peat moss and well-rotted compost or manure.
*Light:* Full sun or partial shade.
*Moisture:* Water only if spring season is dry. Plant is dormant in summer.
*Time to plant:* Fall.
*Planting depth:* 5 to 6 inches.
*Spacing:* 4 to 5 inches apart.
*Care during growing season:* Do not remove foliage until completely withered and brown. Each spring, when shoots emerge, scratch in one tablespoon of 9-9-6 fertilizer per square foot of planting area.
*Bloom time:* Early spring.
*Length of bloom:* 2 weeks.
*Propagation:* It is best to purchase new bulbs; propagating requires considerable expertise.
*Rodent-proof:* No. Very susceptible to rodents that relish not only the foliage aboveground but the bulbs below.
*Forcing:* No.
*Naturalizing:* Although they do not have a tendency to spread significantly, they can be used in a naturalized, woodland setting.
*Endangered species in the wild:* No.

## Recommended Fosteriana (Emperor) Tulips

| CULTIVAR | COLOR |
| --- | --- |
| 'Concerto' | Pure white |
| 'Easter Parade' | Carmine-rose, yellow inside |
| 'Juan' | Orange with yellow base |
| 'Pink Emperor' | Rose-pink |
| 'Princeps' | Bright red |
| 'Red Emperor' | Scarlet |
| 'Sweetheart' | Yellow edged with white |
| 'White Emperor' (synonym 'Purissima') | White |
| 'Yellow Emperor' | Golden yellow |

## Tulipa greigii

Another species tulip, Greigiis are quite similar to Kaufmannianas; however, their blooms are slightly larger. As with Kaufmannianas, Greigiis tend to perennialize. I have seen plantings of 'Red Riding Hood'—an early-spring, low-growing Greigii that sports brilliant red blossoms—bloom in a nearby garden for over fifteen years.

*Type of bulb:* True bulb.
*Color:* Orange, red, yellow, gold, cream-pink, ivory, or combinations thereof.
*Description:* Tulip- or water-lily–shaped blossoms on erect stems over medium green foliage usually mottled with purple or brown.
*Height:* 6 to 20 inches, depending on variety.
*USDA zones:* 3 to 11.
*Soil:* Well drained, ordinary, fortified with sphagnum peat moss and well-rotted compost or manure.
*Light:* Full sun or partial shade.

*'Plaisir,' a low-growing, early-blooming Greigii tulip, sports water-lily-shaped blooms, and is a perfect selection for sparkling color in the rockery or interplanted among the foundation planting.*

*Moisture:* Water only if spring season is dry. Plant is dormant in summer.

*Time to plant:* Fall.

*Planting depth:* 3 to 6 inches.

*Spacing:* 3 to 6 inches apart.

*Care during growing season:* Do not remove foliage until completely withered and brown. Each spring, when shoots emerge, scratch in one tablespoon of 9-9-6 fertilizer per square foot of planting area.

*Bloom time:* Early spring.

*Length of bloom:* 3 weeks.

*Propagation:* It is best to purchase new bulbs; propagating requires considerable expertise.

*Rodent-proof:* No. Very susceptible to rodents that relish not only the foliage aboveground but the bulbs below.

*Forcing:* No.

*Naturalizing:* Although they do not have a tendency to spread significantly, they can be used in a naturalized, woodland setting.

*Endangered species in the wild:* No.

## Recommended Greigii Tulips

| CULTIVARS | COLOR | HEIGHT |
| --- | --- | --- |
| 'Cape Cod' | Orange-red, yellow inside | 12–14″ |
| 'Engadin' | Yellow edged with deep red | 12″ |
| 'Lovely Surprise' | Gold and red | 18″ |
| 'Oriental Splendour' | Lemon edged with carmine-red | 20″ |
| 'Plaisir' | Cream edged with carmine-red | 12″ |
| 'Red Riding Hood' | Brilliant scarlet | 6–8″ |
| 'Royal Splendour' | Scarlet | 20″ |
| 'Scheherazade' | Scarlet | 12″ |
| 'Sweet Lady' | Soft pink and ivory | 8″ |

## *Tulipa kaufmanniana*
### WATER-LILY TULIPS

These species tulips are much lower growing than the Dutch hybrids and Darwins, but they are well suited to rock gardens and doorway gardens. They tend to perennialize, repeating their display year after year.

*Type of bulb:* True bulb.

*Color:* Salmon, scarlet, yellow, cream, apricot, orange, or combinations thereof.

*Description:* Tulip- or water-lily–shaped blossoms held on erect stems over medium green, medium-green-and-burgundy, or medium-green-and-white foliage.

*Height:* 6 to 12 inches, depending on species.

*USDA zones:* 3 to 11.

*Soil:* Well drained, ordinary, fortified with sphagnum peat moss and well-rotted compost or manure.

*Light:* Full sun or partial shade.

*Moisture:* Water only if spring season is dry. Plant is dormant in summer.

*Time to plant:* Fall.

*Planting depth:* 3 to 6 inches.

*Spacing:* 3 to 6 inches apart.

*Care during growing season:* Do not remove foliage until completely withered and brown.

Each spring, when shoots emerge, scratch in one tablespoon of 9-9-6 fertilizer per square foot of planting area.

*Bloom time:* Early spring.

*Length of bloom:* 2 weeks.

*Propagation:* It is best to purchase new bulbs; propagating requires considerable expertise.

*Rodent-proof:* No. Very susceptible to rodents that relish not only the foliage aboveground but the bulbs below.

*Forcing:* No.

*Naturalizing:* Although they do not have a tendency to spread significantly, they can be used in a naturalized, woodland setting.

*Endangered species in the wild:* No.

*Kaufmanniana tulip 'Stresa' is a low-growing, compact plant with brilliant yellow blossoms marked with red coloration.*

## Recommended Kaufmanniana Tulips

| CULTIVAR | COLOR | HEIGHT |
| --- | --- | --- |
| 'Ancilla' | Pink and white | 6" |
| 'Chopin' | Lemon yellow | 6" |
| 'Fritz Kriesler' | Salmon-pink | 6" |
| 'Gold Coin' | Scarlet edged with yellow | 6–8" |
| 'Heart's Delight' | Carmine and rose | 10" |
| 'Shakespeare' | Salmon-orange-apricot | 6–8" |
| 'Showwinner' | Scarlet | 6–8" |
| 'Stresa' | Gold with orange border | 7" |
| 'Vivaldi' | Yellow and crimson | 7" |
| 'Waterlily' | Cream and carmine | 7" |

## *Tulipa* (Dutch)

And here they are, perhaps what you've been waiting for: the glorious Dutch tulips. These bloom early in spring, mid-season, and late; so if you select from each category, you can have almost two months of tulip bloom. Just to sift things out for you, here are the various classifications according to bloom time.

EARLY SPRING: Single early, double early.

MID-SPRING: Mendel, Triumph, Darwin hybrid, double peony, Viridiflora.

LATE SPRING: Darwin, lily-flowering, Cottage, Rembrandt, Parrot, double late.

*Type of bulb:* True bulb.

*Color:* Every color except blue.

*Description:* Single or double turban-shaped flower held on erect stems over medium green broad-leaved foliage.

*Height:* 18 to 30 inches, depending on variety.

*USDA zones:* 3 to 7.

*Soil:* Well drained, ordinary, fortified with sphagnum peat moss and well-rotted compost or manure.

*Light:* Full sun or partial shade.

*Moisture:* Water only if spring season is dry. Plant is dormant in summer.

*Time to plant:* Mid- to late fall.

*The mini-blossoms of* Tulipa dasystemon (*synonym* tarda) *add crisp white and yellow color to the early-spring garden.*

## Mid-Season Blooming Dutch Tulip Cultivars
## Recommended for Perennialization

| CULTIVAR | COLOR | HEIGHT | CULTIVAR | COLOR | HEIGHT |
|---|---|---|---|---|---|
| 'Candela' | Yellow | 12–16″ | 'Merry Widow' | White edged with red | 12–18″ |
| 'Diplomate' | Red | 16–24″ | 'Monte Carlo' | Yellow | 10–15″ |
| 'Frankfurt' | Red | 12–18″ | 'Negrita' | Purple | 12–18″ |
| 'Golden Apeldoorn' | Yellow | 16–24″ | 'Orange Emperor' | Orange | 12–16″ |
| 'Golden Oxford' | Yellow | 16–24″ | 'Oscar' | Red | 12–18″ |
| 'Golden Parade' | Yellow | 16–24″ | 'Oxford' | Red | 16–24″ |
| 'Gudishnik' | Orange fringed with yellow | 16–24″ | 'Princess Victoria' | White edged with red | 16–24″ |
| 'Hoangho' | Yellow | 10–15″ | 'Spring Song' | White edged with red | 16–24″ |
| 'Ile de France' | Red | 14–30″ | 'Striped Apeldoorn' | Red striped with yellow | 16–24″ |
| 'Jewel of Spring' | Red edged with yellow | 16–24″ | 'Yellow Dover' | Yellow | 16–24″ |
| 'Los Angeles' | Yellow with red | 16–24″ | 'Yokohama' | Red edged with yellow | 12–18″ |

## Late-Blooming Dutch Tulip Cultivars
## Recommended for Perennialization

| CULTIVAR | COLOR | HEIGHT | CULTIVAR | COLOR | HEIGHT |
|---|---|---|---|---|---|
| 'Ad Rem' | Yellow edged with red | 16–24″ | 'Jimmy' | Red-orange | 12–18″ |
| 'Burgundy Lace' | Red | 16–30″ | 'Karel Doorman' | Yellow edged with red | 16–20″ |
| 'Delmonte' | Purple fringed with white | 12–18″ | 'Kees Nelis' | Yellow edged with red | 12–18″ |
| 'Don Quichotte' | Red-orange | 12–18″ | 'Makeup' | Red edged with white | 14–30″ |
| 'Duke of Wellington' | White | 14–30″ | 'Orange Bouquet' | Orange | 24–30″ |
| 'Dyanito' | Red | 24–30″ | 'Parade' | Yellow edged with red | 16–24″ |
| 'Gordon Cooper' | Red-orange edged with red | 16–24″ | 'Smiling Queen' | Red-orange edged with pink | 14–30″ |
|  |  |  | 'Sorbet' | Red-orange | 14–30″ |

*Planting depth:* 6 to 8 inches.

*Spacing:* 6 inches apart.

*Care during growing season:* Do not remove foliage until completely withered and brown. Each spring, when shoots emerge, scratch in one tablespoon of 9-9-6 fertilizer per square foot of planting area.

*Bloom time:* Early to late spring, depending on variety.

*Length of bloom:* 2 to 3 weeks, depending on variety.

*Propagation:* It is best to purchase new bulbs; propagating requires considerable expertise.

*Rodent-proof:* No. Very susceptible to rodents that relish not only the foliage aboveground but the bulbs below.

*Forcing:* Yes, some cultivars. See page 137.

*Naturalizing:* No.

*Endangered species in the wild:* No.

The Netherlands Bulb Industry has run trial plantings of specific varieties of Dutch tulips for four years in conjunction with the North Carolina State University Arboretum to test their tendency to perennialize. The cultivars that performed best are listed on the following page. Also, almost all early-season tulips tend to perennialize. Some are readily available from suppliers; others are not so easy to locate. I suggest you refer to the bulb source list on page 144, send for a dozen or so catalogues, go through them, and select from the recommended list.

The trials run by North Carolina State University were planted in zones 7, 8, and 9—among the milder climatic regions of the country. This does not necessarily mean that these tulip varieties will not do as well in cooler zones. However, be advised that in any case, similar results in your garden, no matter where it is, are most assuredly not guaranteed. And although some Darwin, Triumph, Parrot, and double early tulips received high ratings for perennialization, the majority of those with high ratings were the Darwin hybrids.

## *Tulipa* ("Wild" Species)

These irresistible, early-blooming miniature tulips bloom exactly as they do in the wild—and tend to spread. They are well suited for the rock garden or tucked here and there near entrances or

*Tulipa turkestanica is another early-blooming species tulip that is ideal for naturalizing and multiplies readily.*

within view of windows so they can be enjoyed during late winter/early spring days.

*Type of bulb:* True bulb.
*Color:* Yellow, white, red, rose, purple, or combinations thereof.
*Description:* 1- to 2-inch tulip-shaped blossoms held on erect stems over broad, medium green foliage, some twisted.
*Height:* 3 to 18 inches, depending on species.
*USDA zones:* 3 to 11.
*Soil:* Well drained, ordinary, fortified with sphagnum peat moss and well-rotted compost or manure.
*Light:* Full sun or partial shade.
*Moisture:* Water only if spring season is dry. Plant is dormant in summer.
*Time to plant:* Fall.
*Planting depth:* 2 to 3 inches.
*Spacing:* 3 to 4 inches apart.
*Care during growing season:* Do not remove foliage until completely withered and brown. Each spring, when shoots emerge, scratch in one tablespoon of 9-9-6 fertilizer per square foot of planting area.
*Bloom time:* Early spring.
*Length of bloom:* 1 to 3 weeks, depending on species.
*Propagation:* Dig up after foliage withers, remove the small bulbs attached to the larger bulbs, and replant or store over the summer in an airy, cool place and plant in the fall.
*Rodent-proof:* No. Very susceptible to rodents that relish not only the foliage aboveground but the bulbs below.

*Forcing:* No.
*Naturalizing:* Yes. The only tulip variety that truly multiplies year in and year out.
*Endangered species in the wild:* All bulbs sold in this country and Canada are from cultivated stock.

## "Wild" Species Tulips Suitable for the Garden

| SPECIES | COLOR | HEIGHT |
|---|---|---|
| T. bakeri 'Lilac Wonder' | Lilac and yellow | 12″ |
| T. biflora | Yellow and white | 8″ |
| T. chrysantha | Yellow and red | 8″ |
| T. clusiana (Peppermint tulip) | Rose and white | 8″ |
| T. dasystemon (syn. tarda) | Yellow and white | 3–6″ |
| T. hageri | Deep red | 6″ |
| T. patens (Persian tulip) | Yellow and white | 6–9″ |
| T. praestans | Pale red | 12–18″ |
| T. pulchella | Pale purple | 4–6″ |
| T. turkestanica | White with yellow center | 8″ |

*Chapter Five*

# BLOOMING BULBS
# FOR SUMMER

After the spring-blooming bulbs have staged their electrifying show, it is time to prepare, plan, and plant summer-blooming bulbs to accent your landscape plan. Beyond their beautiful and often highly fragrant blossoms, the diverse foliage of summer bulbs lends variety to any planting. Some have medium green, spearlike leaves, others lush, deep green leaves, and still others brilliantly colored variegated foliage with a look of the tropics.

While none of the tender summer bulbs are suitable for naturalizing, the hardy hybrid lilies naturalize quite well in woodland or meadow settings.

All of the summer-blooming bulbs included here, with the exception of the lilies, are tender—that is, they will not survive cold winter temperatures in most areas of the United States and Canada. Almost all must be dug up in the fall, stored over the winter in a cool dry place, and replanted in the spring—except in the warmest areas of the country. Storage instructions are in-

cluded in each tender-bulb entry.

Summer-blooming bulbs are all grown commercially and are not harvested in the wild, so none are endangered in their natural habitat.

## WHERE AND WHEN TO BUY SUMMER-BLOOMING BULBS

Outdoor planting time for most summer bulbs is after all danger of frost has passed in your area. This is the same time that you set out tomato plants. Garden centers and nurseries usually begin to sell the bulbs during mid-spring, but *don't* plant until after the last frost. Some summer-blooming plants—tuberous begonias, caladiums, and colocasia (elephant ears), for example—need a head start and must be started indoors from six to eight weeks before outdoor planting time. They are generally available at local outlets from January through March.

Although more and more varieties of summer bulbs become available locally each year, for the best selection send for the catalogues listed on pages 144–45. Order tuberous begonias, caladiums, and colocasia in January, and the other bulbs in March or April. Mail-order companies almost always ship bulbs at the appropriate planting time for your area.

## *Acidanthera bicolor*
ABYSSINIAN GLADIOLUS, PEACOCK ORCHID

These inexpensive bulbs should be planted more widely than they are. They are very easily grown and exude a heavy, provocative scent, more pronounced during the torpid heat of midsummer evenings. Ideal as a cut flower.

*Type of bulb:* Corm.
*Color:* Creamy white with mahogany-colored center.
*Description:* 2-inch star-shaped blossoms held over medium green spearlike foliage.
*Height:* 1½ to 2 feet.
*USDA zones:* 7 to 11—hardy; 6 and north—dig up in fall and store as directed under "Winter Care."
*Soil:* Average, enriched with sphagnum peat moss and well-rotted compost or manure.
*Light:* Full sun or partial shade.
*Moisture:* Water during prolonged summer drought.
*Time to plant outdoors:* Spring, after all danger of frost.
*Planting depth:* 3 to 4 inches.

*The white-and-mahogany blossoms of* Acidanthera bicolor, *a close relative of the gladiolus, offer not only a touch of class to a summer bulb garden but an evocative scent as well.*

*Spacing:* 4 to 6 inches apart.
*Care during growing season:* Scratch a light dusting of 9-9-6 fertilizer into the soil when leaves emerge and again 3 to 4 weeks later. Stake plants when a foot high.
*Bloom time:* Mid- to late summer.
*Length of bloom:* 2 to 4 weeks.
*Propagation:* In the fall, when the leaves turn brown, dig up the corms, remove the small cormels that have developed, and store over

*Here the formal look of blue African lily* (Agapanthus africanus) *is softened by a nearby planting of a drift of rudbeckia.*

winter. Sow in drills the following spring after the danger of frost has passed. Cormels should bloom after two years. Corms, however, are so reasonable in price that it is hardly worth the trouble to propagate from small cormels.

*Rodent-proof:* Yes.

*Winter care:* In zones 8 to 11, winter over in ground. Elsewhere, dig up corms when the leaves turn brown in fall. Shake off soil and dry for several days in an airy, shady, frost-free place, then cut the tops back to 2 inches and remove the remains of the previous season's corms. Store in dry sphagnum peat moss, perlite, or vermiculite at 55° to 60° F.

## *Agapanthus africanus*
BLUE AFRICAN LILY, LILY OF THE NILE

Because they are not hardy, agapanthus is best used potted and grown in pots or tubs. They are almost always sold and shipped potted, and most will be pot bound—that is, their roots will be crowded in the container, a condition they prefer. In fact, they are more floriferous when pot bound.

*Type of bulb:* Fleshy-rooted rhizome.
*Color:* Sky blue or white.
*Description:* Clusters of 1- to 4-inch blossoms on leafless stems held over medium green mounds of straplike leaves.
*Height:* 12 to 18 inches.
*USDA zones:* 9 to 11—hardy; 8 and north—bring in during fall and winter over as directed under "Winter Care."
*Soil:* When purchased, potted specimens are contained in appropriate soil.
*Light:* Prefers full sun but will flower in partial shade.
*Moisture:* Do not let dry out. Water every other day during season.
*Time to plant or place outdoors:* Spring, after all danger of frost has passed.
*Planting depth:* Sink purchased prepotted plants, pot and all, into the ground until the top of pot is soil level.
*Care during growing season:* Feed every 2 weeks with any soluble houseplant fertilizer at recommended strength or with time-release fertilizer according to label directions.
*Bloom time:* Midsummer.
*Length of bloom:* 4 weeks.
*Propagation:* Repotting or dividing in early spring about every 3 years is recommended. Repot with sandy loam.
*Rodent-proof:* Yes.
*Winter care:* In zones 9 to 11, winter over outdoors. Elsewhere, before first frost, lift pots from the ground or bring terrace pots indoors. Place in a north window and water only enough to keep tips of leaves from drying out. This dormant period is necessary for subsequent year's flowering. Some yellow-

ing of leaves is normal at this time and is a good sign of proper dormancy.

## Anemone

Although summer-flowering St. Brigid and de Caen anemones are best grown professionally in greenhouses, some people have moderate luck growing them in the garden. However, don't expect the same large blooms that you buy as cut flowers from your local florist.

I have tried to grow these flowers three years in a row, carefully following directions provided by experts in Holland, each time selecting a different spot in the garden. The first year, I managed to get two blooms out of twenty-five planted tubers, the second year none, and the third four or five. Needless to say, the results have been disappointing, and I have decided that if I must have anemones, I will buy them from my neighborhood flower shop.

For those dogged individuals who want to try, anemones require very special growing conditions (cool spring, followed by hot summer and shade from noonday sun) that must be satisfied in order to bring them to bloom. These conditions are most apt to be found in the Pacific Northwest. Purchase the clawlike tubers in spring and soak in warm water for forty-eight hours before planting.

*Type of bulb:* Tuber.
*Color:* Pink, red, blue, purple, white, or combinations thereof.
*Description:* 3-inch blossoms held on stalks over low-growing rosettes of serrated foliage.
*Height:* 12 to 18 inches.
*USDA zones:* 9 to 11—hardy; 8 and north—dig up in fall and store as directed under "Winter Care."
*Soil:* Well drained, enriched with well-rotted

compost or manure.

*Light:* Full sun or partial shade, with protection from direct rays of hot afternoon sun.

*Moisture:* Keep well watered throughout growing season.

*Time to plant outdoors:* Spring, after all danger of frost has passed.

*Planting depth:* 2 to 3 inches.

*Spacing:* 8 inches apart.

*Care during growing season:* Provide shade from hot noonday sun. Franz Roozen, the renowned Dutch horticulturist, suggests pinching off the first flower bud that grows from each tuber for more profuse blooms. I tried that and it made little difference in its performance.

*Bloom time:* Throughout the summer.

*Length of bloom:* 1 to 2 weeks.

*Propagation:* Because tubers are very inexpensive, it is best to purchase them as you need them. However, if you wish to propagate your own, dig up and divide tubers in late summer after foliage begins to yellow and store as directed under "Winter Care."

*Rodent-proof:* Yes.

*Winter care:* In zones 9 to 11, winter over in the ground. Elsewhere, dig up in late summer, brush away the soil, and store at 55° to 60° F in dry peat moss, perlite, or vermiculite until the following spring.

## *Begonia tuberhybrida*
### TUBEROUS BEGONIA

These spectacular summer flowers, which thrive under shady conditions, are available in both low-growing bedding varieties and pendulous or hanging varieties that are ideal for creating spectacular baskets and window boxes of cascading color. A newly hybridized cultivar called

*Brilliant red tuberous begonias, interplanted with variegated green-and-white hostas, add dramatic color to a shade garden.*

'Non-Stop' offers profuse bloom during the entire summer and fall.

Begonias were discovered in 1690 in the West Indies by a monk named Charles Plumier. He presented the flower to the then governor of the West Indies, Michael Begon, and thus the name *begonia*. Two centuries later, begonias were brought to England, and then to Belgium by the Ghent horticulturist Louis Van Houtte. Today, although largely exported by the Dutch, almost all begonias are grown in Belgium, where each

August magnificent carpets of them are laid down in the Grand Place of Brussels and a three-day Festival of Begonias takes place in the country village of Lochristi, near Ghent.

Beyond their beauty in the shade garden, begonia blossoms can also be used in indoor flower arrangements. They are perhaps most effective placed floating in a compote or tureen filled with water. At dinnertime, floating candles can be added to create a lovely centerpiece. The tubers should be bought in January or February and stored in a frost-free place until ready to plant.

*Type of bulb:* Tuber.

*Color:* All colors except blue and green.

*Description:* 2- to 5-inch blossoms in camellia, carnation, and picotee shapes.

*Height:* 8 to 18 inches.

*USDA zones:* In all zones, dig up in the fall and store as directed under "Winter Care."

*Soil:* Average, fortified with sphagnum peat moss and well-rotted compost or manure.

*Light:* Prefers light or medium shade. Will not thrive in full sun.

*Moisture:* Keep moist throughout the growing season.

*Pre-outdoor planting instructions:* Start tubers about 8 weeks before last frost date in your area. Plant hollow side up in 4- to 5-inch pots or in 4- to 5-inch-deep trays filled with a planting medium such as Pro-Mix or Reddi-Lite. Barely cover with soil.

Place on a windowsill where the temperature does not fall below 60° F. Cover with paper or clear plastic to promote growth, but remove as soon as growth appears. Water sparingly until growth commences. This may take up to 6 weeks. Root growth beneath the soil's surface will begin earlier.

Once the shoots emerge, development will become more rapid. Provide maximum light but shade from strong direct midday sun. Water regularly, never allowing the soil to dry out.

*Planting depth:* Remove prestarted tubers from pots or trays and plant with the top of the tuber even with the surrounding soil level.

*Spacing in garden:* 10 inches apart.

*Spacing in containers:* 6 inches apart.

*Planting outdoors:* Set out in late spring, when outdoor nighttime temperatures reach 50° F and daytime temperatures 70° F. Select a location that is sheltered from strong winds, as begonias do not thrive under this stressful condition. Plant in semi-shade. Although begonias will thrive in a location receiving early morning or late afternoon sun, they cannot tolerate the hot midday sun.

*Care during growing season:* For those planted in the garden, a 1-inch mulch of peat moss will control weeds, retain moisture, and improve growth quality. Scratch a light dusting of 9-9-6 or 5-10-5 fertilizer into the soil every 2 to 3 weeks until the foliage starts to wither in the fall.

For those planted in hanging baskets, pots, or window boxes, feed with an all-purpose liquid houseplant fertilizer once a month according to label intructions. Stake the plants when stems are a foot high.

*Container planting:* Begonias adapt well to container planting, particularly the pendulous or hanging varieties. To plant a hanging basket, line the inside of a wire or plastic plant basket with a 1- to 2-inch layer of stringy sphagnum or Spanish moss (usually available at garden centers or your local florist)—do not use peat moss because it will not cling together and thus will not contain the plants. Fill the lined basket ⅔ full with a planting medium consisting of ⅓ potting soil, ⅓ peat moss, and ⅓ perlite. Press 3 or 4 prestarted

*Even the house puss agrees that these pink hanging tuberous begonias, interplanted with white impatiens, are a perfect selection for these handsome teak window boxes.*

tubers firmly in place and cover with another ½ inch of the mixture. Place on a shaded porch, a partly shaded terrace, or under trees and water every day or two.

You can also grow hanging begonias in window boxes, as long as they are located in a spot that is shady, such as under a porch roof or window awning. To install a window box planting, line the bottom of the window box with 1½ inches of a drainage material, such as broken flowerpot shards, gravel, or plastic packing "popcorn." Fill the window box to within 1 inch of the top with a planting medium as described above. Set the prestarted tubers on top and cover with another ½ inch of the mixture.

To grow upright varieties in containers, place 1 inch of drainage material in the bottom of a 10- or 12-inch container. Fill to within 1½ inches of the top with the planting medium, set 3 or 4 prestarted tubers on top, and cover with another ½ inch of planting medium. Place in a shady or semi-shady location and water every day or two.

*Bloom time:* From early summer to frost.

*Length of bloom:* Each individual blossom lasts for about 2 weeks; however, others provide continuous bloom throughout the season.

*Propagation:* In late winter or early spring, take cuttings from the shoots that grow from the tubers, dust with rooting hormone powder (available at garden centers and nurseries), and root in small pots filled with horticultural or builder's sand. Provide strong light, but not direct sun, and water just enough to keep evenly moist. In about a month, shoots should root. Then plant outside as directed above.

*Rodent-proof:* Yes.

*Winter care:* In all zones, when the plants die back to the ground in the fall, but before the first frost, dig up the tubers. Do not remove the soil. Allow to dry in an airy, shady, frost-free place for several weeks until the steams break away easily. Remove the soil, dust the tubers with a combination fungicide-insecticide, and store in bags of dry sphagnum peat moss, perlite, or vermiculite at 40° to 50° F until January or February, and plant again indoors as directed above.

## Caladium

Caladiums are grown for their spectacular foliage and are especially suited to shady areas of the garden. They provide lush growth and bring the look of the tropics to a summer garden; they are, in fact, native to the rain forests of the Western Hemisphere. Although they sport exotic blooms, these are quite insignificant compared to the foliage. Caladiums can be grown in the garden as well as in containers and window boxes. Many gardeners who grow them in containers bring them indoors long before the first frost and winter them as attractive houseplants. The variegated foliage can also be used in indoor summer flower arrangements. Buy the tubers in January or February and store in a frost-free place until ready to plant.

*Type of bulb:* Tuber.

*Color:* Scores of combinations of red, pink, silver, white, and green foliage. Small, insignificant flowers.

*Description:* Heart or spear-shaped foliage.

*Height:* 6 to 24 inches.

*USDA zones:* 10 and 11—hardy; 9 and north—dig up in the fall and store as directed under "Winter Care."

*Soil:* Moist, fortified with sphagnum peat moss and well-rotted compost or manure.

*Light:* Prefers partial or deep shade. Will not thrive in full sun.

*Moisture:* Keep well watered during the growing season.

*Pre-outdoor planting instructions:* Start tubers about 8 weeks before the last frost date in your area. Plant 2 inches deep in 5- to 6-inch pots or 4- to 5-inch-deep trays filled with premoistened peat moss, leaf mold, or vermiculite.

Water sparingly and place in warm spot (70° to 85° F), out of direct sunlight. Cover with paper or clear plastic to promote growth, but remove as soon as growth appears; this may take up to 6 weeks. Root growth beneath the soil's surface will begin earlier.

Once the shoots emerge, development will become more rapid. Provide maximum light but shade from strong direct midday sun. Water regularly, never allowing the soil to dry out.

*Planting depth:* Remove prestarted tubers from

pots or trays and plant with the top of the tuber even with the surrounding soil level.

*Spacing in garden:* 12 inches apart.

*Spacing in containers:* 8 inches apart.

*Planting outdoors:* Set out in late spring when outdoor nighttime temperatures reach 50° F and outdoor daytime temperatures 70° F. Select a location sheltered from strong winds, as caladiums do not thrive under this stressful condition. Plant in semi-shade. Although caladiums will thrive in a location receiving early morning or late afternoon sun, they

*Pink-and-green caladiums are a welcome relief to the predominantly green colors of this shaded summer hosta garden.*

will not tolerate hot midday sun.

*Care during growing season:* For those planted in the garden, a 1-inch mulch of peat moss will control weeds, retain moisture, and improve growth quality. Make sure, however, that the peat moss is never allowed to dry out. Scratch a light dusting of 9-6-6 or 5-10-5 fertilizer into the soil every 2 to 3 weeks until the foliage starts to wither in the fall.

For those planted in containers or window boxes, feed with all-purpose liquid houseplant fertilizer once a month according to the label directions. Stake plants when the stems are a foot high.

*Container planting:* Caladiums adapt well to container and window-box planting, as long as they are located in a shady spot, out of the scorching midday sun. To install in a container planting, line the bottom inch of a container that is at least 8 inches in diameter or a window box with drainage material, such as broken flowerpot shards, gravel, or plastic packing "popcorn." Fill the container half full of a planting medium consisting of ⅓ potting soil, ⅓ peat moss, and ⅓ perlite. Set the prestarted tubers on top and cover with another 2 inches of the planting medium. Water every day or two.

*Length of bloom:* All season until frost.

*Propagation:* In late winter, when you prestart the caladiums, cut the tubers into pieces, leaving at least one eye, or bud, on each section. If you cut each tuber into pieces with 3 to 5 eyes, fuller plants with several stems will grow. Dust all cut surfaces with a fungicide to prevent decay and let dry for three days. Then plant indoors as directed above.

*Rodent-proof:* Yes.

*Winter care:* In zones 9 and north, dig up the tubers when the plants die back to the ground in the fall, but before the first frost.

(It is a good idea to dig caladiums in zones 10 and 11 as well, although plants will not be affected by frost. This is because a rest period is beneficial.) Do not remove the soil. Allow to dry in an airy, shady, frost-free place for about 1 week, until the foliage comes off with a gentle pull. Remove the soil, dust the tubers with a combination fungicide-insecticide, and store in bags of dry sphagnum peat moss, perlite, or vermiculite at 40° to 50° F until January or February, and replant indoors as directed above.

Caladiums can be wintered over indoors in pots, so bring them inside before the first frost and grow in bright, indirect sunlight during the day; don't allow night temperatures to fall below 65° to 70° F.

## Canna

Spectacular to the point of being garish, cannas will indeed brighten up the dreariest landscape. However, be very careful in selecting the varieties you wish to grow, as even a small planting will overwhelm almost any garden. Shop carefully and select the dwarf varieties (Pfitzer Hybrids, Seven Dwarfs), which are more in scale with the average garden. Also remember that although the screaming reds, oranges, and yellows look inviting in garden catalogues and even attractive in large public parks, the more subdued pinks, creams, and whites are far more suitable for a home garden. Cannas are also suitable for tub or container plantings.

*Type of bulb:* Rhizome.

*Color:* Red, orange, yellow, pink, cream, white, or bicolors.

*Description:* 4- to 5-inch blossoms on spikes held

over broad bright green, blue-green, or
bronze leaves.

*Height:* 1½ to 6 feet, depending on the cultivar.

*USDA zones:* 7 to 11—hardy; 6 and north—dig
up in fall and store as directed under "Winter Care."

*Soil:* Ordinary, generously enriched with sphagnum peat moss and well-rotted compost or
manure.

*Light:* Full sun.

*Moisture:* Water regularly throughout the growing season; cannas like lots of water.

*Time to plant outdoors:* Spring, after all danger of
frost has passed.

*Planting in containers:* In spring, 6 weeks before
the last frost, start the rhizomes in containers that have a planting medium consisting of
one part peat moss, one part potting soil,
and one part builder's or horticultural sand
or perlite and a tablespoon of ground lime.
Move outdoors after all danger of frost has
passed and bring indoors before the first
frost of fall.

*Planting depth:* 1 to 2 inches.

*Spacing:* 15 to 18 inches apart.

*Care during growing season:* Scratch a light dusting of 9-9-6 fertilizer into the soil every 2
weeks during growing season.

*Bloom time:* Mid- to late summer.

*Length of bloom:* 6 weeks.

*Propagation:* Divide rhizomes in spring.

*Rodent-proof:* Yes.

*Winter care:* In zones 7 to 11, winter over in
ground. Elsewhere, cut stalks to ground after blackened by frost. Dig up the roots,
clean off soil, and dry in an airy, shady,
frost-free place for a few days. Store upside
down in dry peat moss, perlite, or vermiculite at 50° to 60° F.

## Recommended Cannas

| CULTIVARS | COLOR | HEIGHT |
|---|---|---|
| Grand Opera Series | White, yellow, pink, scarlet, orange, salmon | 3–4' |
| Pfitzer Hybrids | White, yellow, pink, scarlet, orange, salmon | 2' |
| Seven Dwarfs | White, yellow, pink, scarlet, orange, salmon | 1½' |

## Colocasia
### ELEPHANT'S EAR, TARO, DASHEEN

Grown for their foliage, these massive plants
add an exotic, very tropical ambiance to a shady
garden.

The roots of the plant are used as food in tropical
Asia as well as on the Pacific and Caribbean is-
lands. Hawaiian poi is made by pounding the
cooked roots to a paste. Elephant's ear can also
be grown in large containers, dressing up terraces
and patios with its lush foliage. Buy the tubers in
January or February and store in a frost-free place
until ready to plant.

*Type of bulb:* Tuber.

*Color:* Medium green foliage with insignificant
yellow flowers.

*Description:* Immense elephant-ear-shaped
leaves, sometimes measuring 2 by 1½ feet.

*Height:* 4 to 6 feet.

*USDA zones:* 10 and 11—hardy; 9 and north—
dig up in the fall and store as directed under
"Winter Care."

*Soil:* Moist, fortified with sphagnum peat moss
and well-rotted compost or manure.

*Colocasia, or elephant's ear, is well suited for container planting and brings a touch of the sultry tropics to this deck.*

*Light:* Full sun or partial shade.

*Moisture:* Keep well watered during the growing season.

*Pre-outdoor planting instructions:* Start the large tubers about 8 weeks before the last frost date in your area. Plant at soil level in 6-inch pots filled with premoistened peat moss, leaf mold, or vermiculite. Water sparingly and place in a warm spot (70° to 85° F) out of direct sunlight. Cover with paper or clear plastic to promote growth but remove as soon as growth appears; this may take up to 6 weeks. Root growth beneath the soil's surface will begin earlier.

Once the shoots emerge, development will become more rapid. Provide maximum light but shade from strong direct midday sun. Water regularly, never allowing the soil to dry out.

*Planting depth:* Remove prestarted tubers from pots and plant 4 inches deep.

*Spacing in garden:* 2 to 4 feet apart.

*Spacing in containers:* Plant one tuber per container.

*Planting outdoors:* Set out in late spring, when outdoor nighttime temperatures reach 60° F and outdoor daytime temperatures reach 70° F. Select a sunny or partially shaded location that is sheltered from strong winds; colocasia does not thrive under this stressful condition.

*Care during growing season:* For those planted in the garden, a 1-inch mulch of peat moss will control weeds, retain moisture, and improve growth quality. Do not, however, let the peat moss ever dry out. Scratch a light dusting of 9-6-6 or 5-10-5 fertilizer into the soil every 2 to 3 weeks until the foliage starts to wither in the fall.

For those planted in containers or window boxes, feed with an all-purpose liquid houseplant fertilizer once a month according to the label directions. Stake plants when the stems are a foot high.

*Container planting:* Start in large tubs at least 12 inches deep and 12 inches in diameter in late winter. Fill the bottom inch of the container with drainage material, such as broken flowerpot shards, gravel, or plastic packing "popcorn." Then fill it half full of a planting medium made of ⅓ potting soil, ⅓ peat moss, and ⅓ well-rotted compost or manure. Set the prestarted tubers on top and cover with 2 to 3 inches of the planting medium. Water every day or two. Colocasia can be wintered over indoors in tubs, so bring them inside before the first frost and grow in bright, indirect sunlight during the day; don't allow nighttime temperatures to fall below 65° to 70° F.

*Propagation:* In late winter, when you prestart colocasia, cut the tubers into pieces, leaving at least one eye, or bud, on each division. Dust all cut surfaces with a fungicide to prevent decay and let dry for 3 days. Then plant indoors as directed above.

*Rodent-proof:* Yes.

*Winter care:* In zones 10 and 11, winter over in the ground. Elsewhere, dig up the tubers before the first frost. Do not remove the soil. Allow to dry in an airy, shady, frost-free place for about 1 week or until the foliage comes off with a gentle pull. Remove the soil and store in bags of dry sphagnum peat moss, perlite, or vermiculite at 55° to 60° F until January or February; replant as directed above.

## Crocosmia, syn. *Montbretia*

These charming cousins of the gladiola are more suited to the average garden because their growth habit is loose and informal, rather than stiff, and their blossoms are loosely arranged on the stalks.

*Type of bulb:* Corm.
*Color:* Yellow, orange, or scarlet.
*Description:* 1½-inch blooms held on stalks over medium green spearlike foliage.
*Height:* 2 to 4 feet.

One of the "trendy" bulbs, Crocosmia 'Lucifer' is fast becoming a staple in elegant gardens.

*USDA zones:* 8 to 11—hardy; 7 and north—dig up after frost and store as directed under "Winter Care."
*Soil:* Ordinary.
*Light:* Full sun.
*Moisture:* Water during prolonged summer drought.
*Time to plant outdoors:* Spring, after all danger of frost has passed.
*Planting depth:* 2 inches.
*Spacing:* 3 inches apart.
*Care during growing season:* Scratch a light dusting of 9-9-6 fertilizer into the soil when plants emerge and also 3 to 4 weeks later. Stake plants when a foot high.
*Bloom time:* Late summer/early fall.
*Propagation:* In fall, when leaves turn brown, dig up corms, remove the small cormels, and store over the winter as described under "Winter Care." Sow in drills the following

spring. Cormels should bloom after 2 years. Bulbs, however, are so reasonable in price that it is hardly worth the trouble to propagate from small cormels.

*Rodent-proof:* Yes.

*Winter care:* In zones 8 to 11, winter over in ground. Elsewhere, dig up after frost nips the tops of plants. Leave the soil on the corms and dry for several days in an airy, shady, frost-free place. Store with the soil on the corms in dry sphagnum peat moss, perlite, or vermiculite at 50° to 55° F.

## Dahlia

These spectacular plants have had their ups and downs in popularity. During the early part of this century, the large saucer-sized dahlias were grown in many gardens, both large and small. Today, these are considered far too large for the garden and smaller varieties are more popular. The world of dahlias is a complex one, with many different kinds available. In fact, there are over sixteen different classifications, each of which spans the full range of color, height, and blossom size. They are:

- *Anemone-flowered.* These look like pincushion clusters of tiny tubular flowers, surrounded by a single row of flat petals.
- *Ball.* Ball-shaped blossoms, 4 or more inches in diameter.
- *Cactus-flowered.* Petals are rolled or quill-shaped.
- *Incurved cactus.* Petals curve inward instead of radiating outward as in cactus-flowered.
- *Semicactus.* Petals are tubelike for a third of their length.
- *Straight cactus.* Petals are tubelike for half their length.

- *Collarette.* Single row of petals around an inner row of shorter petals in a different color.
- *Dwarf.* Up to 2½ feet tall with a profusion of 2- to 4-inch blossoms with a single row of petals.
- *Decorative.* Petals are long, of equal length, and symmetrical.
- *Informal decorative.* Petals are long, twisted, and irregularly spaced.
- *Miniature.* Four feet high with 2½- to 4½-inch blossoms in all dahlia shapes except ball and pompon.
- *Miniature ball.* Ball-shaped blossoms less than 4 inches in diameter.
- *Orchid.* Star-shaped blossoms with open centers.
- *Peony.* Peonylike blossoms.
- *Pompon.* Blossoms not as round as ball dahlias and only 2 inches across.
- *Single.* Blossoms have open centers with a surrounding row of petals.

In mail-order catalogues offering dahlias, the classes aren't often included, but blossom size usually is, using the following key: A—more than 8 inches across; B—from 6 to 8 inches across; BB—from 4 to 6 inches across; and M—less than 4 inches across.

When you cut dahlias for indoor flower arrangements, dip the ends of the stems into an inch of boiling water for a second or sear the ends with a flame to prolong flower life.

*Type of bulb:* Tuberous root.
*Color:* Every color except blue and true green. Many multicolors.
*Description:* Blossoms range from less than an inch to over a foot in diameter and are held on stiff, erect stems held over lush, dark green serrated foliage.

*Because they are low-growing and their myriad blossoms are small, mini-dahlias, in this case the anemone form 'Magic Carpet,' are better suited for the average garden than the taller, more flamboyantly colored varieties. Here they are set amid a planting of the pale purple annual* Gomphrena globosa.

*Height:* 1 to 7 feet, depending on variety.

*USDA zones:* 10 and 11—although plant is hardy, it is preferable to dig up after bloom season and store as directed under "Winter Care." 9 and north—dig up in fall and store.

*Soil:* Well drained, liberally enriched with sphagnum peat moss and well-rotted compost or manure.

*Light:* Full sun but will grow in partial shade, although not as well.

*Moisture:* Keep well watered all through the season. Place a 2-inch mulch of rotted compost or wood chips over the planting to conserve moisture.

*Time to plant outdoors:* Spring, after all danger of frost has passed.

*Spacing:* Taller varieties (over 4 feet): 4 to 5 feet apart. Shorter varieties: 1 foot apart.

*Planting instructions:*

TALLER VARIETIES (OVER 4 FEET): Dig a hole 1 foot deep by 1 foot wide. Work ¼ cup of 9-9-6 fertilizer into the bottom of the hole.

Drive a 5- to 6-foot stake into the bottom of the hole (this supports the plant as it grows). Set one tuberous root in the bottom of the hole with the stem end facing up. Spread its roots like the hands of a clock. Cover with 3 inches of soil and water thoroughly.

As the shoots grow, gradually fill in the hole with soil. When 6 inches tall, thin out all but one or two of the shoots. When these shoots have three pairs of leaves, pinch out the growing tip just above the upper set of leaves to encourage bushy growth. Pinch again after subsequent growth has produced three more pairs of leaves.

SHORTER VARIETIES: Dig a hole 6 inches deep by 6 inches wide and work ¼ cup 9-9-6 fertilizer into the bottom of the hole. Staking is unnecessary with shorter varieties. Set one tuberous root in the bottom of the hole with the stem end facing up. Spread its roots like the hands of a clock. Cover with 2 inches of soil and water thoroughly.

As the shoots grow, gradually fill in the hole with soil. When 3 inches tall, thin out all but four or five of the shoots. When these shoots have two pairs of leaves, pinch out the growing tip just above the upper set of leaves to encourage bushy growth. It is not necessary to pinch shorter varieties again.

*Care during growing season:* Scratch a light dusting of 9-9-6 fertilizer into the soil when the plants are well established and water thoroughly.

*Bloom time:* Midsummer to frost.

*Length of bloom:* 2 weeks.

*Propagation:* Divide clumps with a sharp knife, making sure that each separate root is attached to a portion of stalk with a visible growth eye. This can be done in the fall after digging and preparing for winter storage or in the spring, 2 to 4 weeks before outdoor planting time. If you divide in the fall, you can easily recognize the eyes and storing smaller roots is easier, but they are more likely to shrivel in storage and are more susceptible to rot. If you do divide in the fall, dust each cut with fungicide or sulphur to prevent rot during storage. Either way, place the divided roots in moist sand to plump them up and encourage sprouting after dividing and before planting.

*Rodent-proof:* Yes.

*Winter care:* All zones, when stalks have yellowed or been nipped by frost, dig a 2-foot-

*The pale orange color of 'Border Princess,' a cactus-flowering dahlia, provides an offbeat contrast, à la the paintings of Gauguin, to the deep magenta of these native geraniums.*

diameter circle around the plant and gently pry up with a pitchfork. Shake off any loose soil, being careful not to break roots. Let the clump dry in the sun for several hours, then gently remove loose soil. Place the roots in a single layer in a plastic-lined box and cover with dry sand, peat moss, vermiculite, perlite, or sawdust. Store in a dark, dry, cool (40° to 45° F) place until spring. Check occasionally during the winter for signs of shriveling, lightly moistening the storage material if necessary.

## Gladiolus

A flower that unfortunately is associated with funerals, gladiolas are perhaps best grown in the cutting garden and used to add dramatic vertical touches to indoor flower arrangements. There are, however, several species of gladiolas that deserve to be more widely planted (see pages 94–95 for a listing). In addition to being more in scale with the average garden, and bearing spikes of flowers that are loosely arranged on the stalks, they are hardy and don't need to be dug up and stored over the winter.

*Type of bulb:* Corm.
*Color:* All colors of the rainbow.
*Description:* Columns of blossoms on stalks with medium green spearlike foliage.
*Height:* 1 to 5 feet, depending on the cultivar or species.
*USDA zones:* 8 to 11—hardy, but for best blooming results, dig up and store; 7 and north—dig up in fall and store as described under "Winter Care."
*Soil:* Light, sandy loam is preferred but will grow in ordinary soil enriched with sphagnum peat moss and well-rotted compost. Avoid

*The new mini-gladiolas are shorter and looser in appearance than the tall, stiff standard varieties and are better suited to a mixed border. The soft white and pink of this ruffled gladiolus 'Friendship' can be used effectively in many indoor summer flower arrangements.*

using manures; they can cause bulb rot.
*Light:* Full sun.
*Moisture:* Water regularly during prolonged summer drought.
*Time to plant outdoors:* Spring, after all danger of frost has passed.
*Planting depth:* 4 to 6 inches.
*Spacing:* 4 to 6 inches apart.

*Care during growing season:* Scratch a light dusting of 9-9-6 fertilizer into the soil when plants emerge and again 3 to 4 weeks later. Stake plants when they're a foot high.

*Bloom time:* Throughout summer and fall, depending on planting dates.

*Length of bloom:* 2 weeks.

*Propagation:* In fall, when leaves turn brown, dig up corms, remove the small cormels from the larger corms, and store separately over the winter as directed under "Winter Care." Sow in drills the following spring after the threat of frost. Cormels should bloom after 2 years. However, corms are so reasonable in price, it is hardly worth the trouble to propagate from small cormels.

*Rodent-proof:* Yes.

*Winter care:* For tender glads, dig up after blooming (in zones 10 and 11) or when frost nips the tops of the plants (in other zones). Leave the soil on the corms and dry for several days in an airy, shady, frost-free place. Store with the soil still on the corms in dry sphagnum peat moss, perlite, or vermiculite to 50° to 55° F. Hardy species of glads can winter over in the ground.

## Recommended Gladiolas

The following are different varieties of *Gladiolus hybridus* that are available through mail-order sources or at your local garden center or nursery at planting time.

### THE ROYALTY GROUP (GROWS TO A HEIGHT OF 3 TO 5 FEET)

| CULTIVAR | COLOR |
| --- | --- |
| 'Chantilly Lace' | Ruffled pink |
| 'China Girl' | Rose with white throat |

| CULTIVAR | COLOR |
| --- | --- |
| 'Foxy Lady' | Bright red |
| 'Gold Coin' | Gold |
| 'Greenland' | Pale green |
| 'Hallmark' | White with ruby markings |
| 'Lavender Ruffles' | Pink-lavender |
| 'Mandrake' | Rose with gold throat |
| 'Royal Blush' | Deep purple |
| 'Sandalwood' | Brown with gold center |

### THE GIANT GROUP (GROWS TO A HEIGHT OF 4 TO 5 FEET)

| CULTIVAR | COLOR |
| --- | --- |
| 'Beverly Ann' | Lavender |
| 'Early Green' | Green |
| 'Early Yellow' | Yellow |
| 'Friendship' | Light pink |
| 'Golden Scepter' | Gold |
| 'Intrepid' | Scarlet |
| 'Jacksonville Gold' | Deep gold |
| 'Jester' | Ruffled yellow with red blotch |
| 'Nova Lux' | Lemon yellow |
| 'Peter Pears' | Soft orange |
| 'Plum Tart' | Deep purple |
| 'Priscilla' | White with lavender markings |
| 'Rose Supreme' | Rose |
| 'Saxony' | Orange-red |
| 'Spic and Span' | Salmon |
| 'Trader Horn' | Scarlet |
| 'White Friendship' | Ruffled white |
| 'White Prosperity' | White |
| 'Wig's Sensation' | Ruffled Red |
| 'Wine & Roses' | Rose, purple, or white |

## THE BUTTERFLY GROUP (GROWS TO A HEIGHT OF 4 TO 6 FEET)

| CULTIVAR | COLOR |
| --- | --- |
| 'Blackpool' | Gold with red blotch |
| 'Eastbourne' | Purple with red blotch |
| 'Georgette' | Red with yellow blotch |
| 'Green Bird' | Ivory with chartreuse blotch |
| 'Hypnose' | Pink or yellow |
| 'Mademoiselle de Paris' | Scarlet with cream center |
| 'Merry' | Coral or red with yellow blotch |
| 'Richmond' | White with red blotch |

## THE TINY TOT GROUP (GROWS TO A HEIGHT OF 2 TO 3 FEET)

| CULTIVAR | COLOR |
| --- | --- |
| 'Aglow' | Ruffled red |
| 'Fiesta' | Salmon-orange-yellow |
| 'Golden Nugget' | Ruffled yellow |
| 'Irish Linen' | Green |
| 'Jackpot' | Pink or white |
| 'Littlest Angel' | White with yellow throat |
| 'Smarty' | Bronze with brown blotches |
| 'Trump' | Deep red |

## *Recommended Hardy Gladiolas*

| SPECIES | ZONES | COLOR | HEIGHT |
| --- | --- | --- | --- |
| G. blandus | 7–11 | Pink | 12–18" |
| G. byzantinus | 5–11 | Red | 2' |
| G. x colvillei | 7–11 | Red with yellow undermarkings | 18' |
| G. tristis | 7–11 | Creamy white | 18" |

## *Gloriosa*
### GLORY LILY, CLIMBING LILY

This lovely lily is not difficult to grow and should be planted in more gardens than it is. Gloriosas can also be grown as houseplants. To do this, pot in spring in a mixture of one part peat moss, one part packaged potting soil, and one part horticultural sand or perlite with a teaspoon of ground limestone mixed in. Place in a window that receives four hours of sunlight a day, water regularly, and feed once a month with any houseplant fertilizer according to the directions. In the fall or winter, when the flowers fade, do not water or feed; allow the plant to go dormant. Begin watering and fertilizing again in the spring for the new season's growth.

*Type of bulb:* Tuber.
*Color:* Yellow or orange petals tipped with red or scarlet.
*Description:* 3- to 4-inch blossoms on vines with rich green oval leaves.
*Height:* Usually 3 to 4 feet, but can reach 6 feet in very rich soil.
*USDA zones:* 8 to 11—hardy; 7 and north—dig up in fall and store as directed under "Winter Care."
*Soil:* Ordinary, enriched with sphagnum peat moss and well-rotted compost or manure.
*Light:* Full sun or light shade.
*Moisture:* Keep well watered during the growing season.
*Time to plant outdoors:* Spring, after all danger of frost has passed.
*Planting depth:* 4 to 5 inches.
*Spacing:* 8 to 12 inches apart.
*Care during growing season:* As plant grows, provide support, such as a small trellis or fence. Each month, scratch in a dusting of 9-9-6 fertilizer and water.

*Although it takes some experience and care to successfully grow gloriosa lilies, these climbers look spectacular grown on a small trellis.*

*Bloom time:* Midsummer.
*Length of bloom:* 2 weeks.
*Propagation:* Divide tubers in spring or separate small tubers that develop beside large ones when you dig up tubers in the fall.
*Rodent-proof:* Yes.
*Winter care:* In zones 8 to 11, winter over in ground. Elsewhere, dig up before first frost, clean off the soil, dry for several days in an airy, shady, frost-free place, and store at 55° to 60° F in dry peat moss, perlite, or vermiculite.

## *Hymenocallis,* syn. *Ismene*
### SPIDER LILY, PERUVIAN DAFFODIL

The blossoms on the hymenocallis are utterly breathaking; however, it is difficult to bring these bulbs to bloom. I tried a number of times and had mild success only once. I was told that it often takes two or three years of nurturing the plant during the growing season, digging it up in the fall, storing it during the winter, and replanting it in the spring to secure bloom. I did that once, planted in spring, got no bloom that year, dug and stored over the winter, and replanted the following spring—still no bloom. At any rate, here are the growing instructions. I hope you have more luck than I did.

*Type of bulb:* True bulb.
*Color:* White or yellow.
*Description:* Delicate, 3- to 4-inch blossoms, resembling spiders, atop stalks with medium green straplike foliage.
*Height:* 18 to 24 inches.
*USDA zones:* 8 to 11—hardy; 7 and north—dig up in fall and store as directed under "Winter Care."
*Soil:* Ordinary, enriched with sphagnum peat moss and well-rotted compost or manure.
*Light:* Full sun or partial shade.
*Moisture:* Water regularly during prolonged summer drought.
*Time to plant outdoors:* Spring, after all danger of frost has passed.
*Planting depth:* 3 to 5 inches.
*Spacing:* 9 to 12 inches apart.
*Care during growing season:* Scratch a light dusting of 9-9-6 fertilizer into the soil when leaves emerge and again six weeks later.
*Bloom time:* Mid- to late summer.
*Propagation:* In the fall, when you dig bulbs to winter over, remove smaller bulbs that have formed around larger ones and store as directed under "Winter Care."
*Rodent-proof:* Yes.
*Winter care:* In zones 8 to 11, winter over in ground. Elsewhere, in fall, before frost, dig clumps and dry in an airy, shady, frost-free

*Peruvian daffodils* (Hymenocallis) *are summer-blooming bulbs which add elegance to any flower arrangement and offer a haunting scent.*

place until leaves turn brown. Cut off leaves and store bulbs upside down in dry sphagnum peat moss, perlite, or vermiculite at 65° to 70° F.

## Lilium

Lilies are among the few hardy summer-flowering bulbs. A vast variety is available, so you must carefully select those that will best suit your garden and property. You can use lilies in perennial borders and island beds, for masses of color among shrub borders, or incorporated within foundation plantings to add zest to their usual monotony. They are ideal for bouquets and cut-flower arrangements, are highly fragrant, and, as a delightful bonus, attract hummingbirds.

When cutting lilies for bouquets or to give as gifts, it is best to remove the stamens from the bloom—the pollen on them can stain fabric. Simply cut the stamens with scissors or pinch them off with your fingers. Try to be careful not to let any pollen fall on the flower petals; it detracts from the beauty of the bloom. If you do decide to pick an entire bouquet of lilies to place in the house, the scent may be too overwhelming, indeed funereal. It is probably better to mix one or two stalks of lilies with other flowers.

*Type of bulb:* True bulb.
*Color:* All colors except blue.
*Description:* Depending on species, star and trumpet shapes with 4- to 8-inch blossoms held on stalks that also bear glossy, dark green leaves.
*Height:* 2 to 8 feet, depending on species.
*USDA zones:* 3 to 11.
*Soil:* Ordinary, enriched with sphagnum peat moss and well-rotted compost or manure.
*Light:* Full sun to partial shade.
*Moisture:* Water well during prolonged summer drought.
*Time to plant outdoors:* Spring is best, but you can also plant in summer or fall.
*Planting depth:* 6 to 8 inches.
*Spacing:* Small bulbs: 6 inches apart; large bulbs (those the size of a fist): 18 inches apart.
*Planting instructions:* Fortify the soil before planting. Dig a hole 1 foot across and 1 foot deep and mix a handful of all-purpose 9-9-6 fertilizer in the bottom of the hole. It is a

*Towering Madonna lilies* (Lilium candidum) *add an authentic touch to this contemporary version of a medieval herb garden.*

good idea to mix about one tablespoon of an acid-type fertilizer such as Miracid into the hole as well. Plant the bulbs, tamp down the soil, and water thoroughly. After planting, mulch heavily (about 2 inches), as lilies thrive in cool, moist soil.

*Care during growing season:* As the flower stalks grow, taller-growing varieties will have to be staked. To do this, drive a 1-inch-by-2-inch wooden stake about 6 feet tall into the soil next to the lily. Take care not to drive the stake too close to the stalk, as you might injure the bulb. Tie the stalk to the stake

with twine, preferably green in color, so that it does not show. Shorter varieties usually do not need staking. After blooming, remove the spent blossoms. In fall, after the killing frost, remove the withered stalks. If you cut lilies for bouquets, do not cut long stems— the food for next year's bloom is contained in the stems and leaves of the plant. Renew the mulch each year to ensure cool growing conditions for the roots. Each spring, scratch a handful of acid-type fertilizer around the base of each plant.

*Pests and diseases:* Lilies are almost totally pest-

and disease-free, though aphids might occasionally attack. The best thing to do in this case is to spray the stalks with water from a hose to dislodge them. If the problem persists, dust with rotenone, available at garden centers and nurseries, or spray with any indoor or outdoor house and garden spray.

*Bloom time:* Mid- to late summer, depending on the species.

*Length of bloom:* 2 to 4 weeks, depending on the species.

*Propagation:* If the plants become crowded, dig them up after blooming, separate the bulbs, and plant as described above.

Lilies can also be propagated from the scales that encircle the bulbs or, in the case of only one species, *L. tigrinum splendens*, from the small bulbils that form around the stems.

To propagate from scales, in midsummer, after bloom, dig up the bulb and remove the outer scales. Be sure not to remove more than half of the scales on the bulb. Replant the bulb. Dust the scales with a fungicide (available at garden centers and nurseries) and place them, in layers and spaced well apart, on slightly moist vermiculite or perlite in a plastic bag. Seal the bag and store at 68° to 72° F for 6 to 8 weeks. After this time, you will notice that tiny bulblets have developed on each scale. Place the bag in the refrigerator for the winter or store in a winter cold frame. Plant in the nursery in the spring and leave there for 2 years. The third spring, when they are mature enough to flower, plant in a permanent spot.

To propagate from bulbils, remove them when they are ripe and can be broken off easily, around midsummer. Plant 1 inch deep in a medium of equal portions of potting soil or garden loam, coarse sand, and peat moss.

Place in a cold frame over the winter. In the spring, when shoots emerge, plant in the nursery and leave there for 2 years. The third spring, when they are mature enough to flower, plant in a permanent spot.

*Rodent-proof:* No.

*Some available lily varieties:* The array of lilies available can be overwhelming when you sit down to make a selection for your garden. It took me many years to figure out which ones were best suited to my purposes, and I made a number of mistakes in the process. For example, because I had a location ideally suited to the growing of lilies, those I selected—the Aurelian hybrids—which were supposed to grow to about 4 feet, reached a towering 7 feet and looked absurd in their surroundings. Staking was impossible because I did not have an old telephone pole available. Hence, the lilies flopped about and the stems drooped pitifully from the weight of the blossoms. The following breakdown should help you make selections appropriate for your garden.

• **Aurelian hybrid lilies:** These are the towering trumpet lilies that can grow to 7 or 8 feet. They look magnificent as a backdrop for a very wide border, but for most landscape purposes they are simply too tall. If conditions are less than ideal—that is, if they are planted in full sun and left without mulch—they will dwarf. However, this is best left to more experienced gardeners who have the time and are willing to make the effort to experiment with different locations for lily plants. They bloom from the end of June to the end of July in most areas of the country. This variety always needs staking.

| CULTIVAR | DESCRIPTION | HEIGHT |
|---|---|---|
| 'African Queen' | Huge, deep orange-gold, trumpet-shaped blossoms | 4–7' |
| 'Golden Splendour' | 8 to 20 rich gold, trumpet-shaped flowers per stalk | 5–7' |
| 'Green Magic' | 8 to 20 white with pale green overtone trumpet-shaped flowers per stalk | 4' |
| 'Pink Perfection' | Huge, 8- to 10-inch rich pink trumpet-shaped blossoms | 5–7' |
| 'Regale' | Large blooms of white with gold throats | 4–7' |

*Hybrid 'Haydee' lilies offer bright yellow clusters of bloom, but should be overplanted with daylilies or other perennials to hide their stalks and foliage once they have completed their bloom cycle.*

• **Hybrid lilies:** These are much more manageable and sensible for the average home landscape than the Aurelian hybrids, as these grow from two to four feet, depending on the variety. The flower spike is compact with many blooms, some in solid colors, others speckled. They bloom from mid-June to mid-July in most parts of the country and rarely need staking. Be very careful when selecting colors; some can be quite startling, even garish.

| CULTIVAR | DESCRIPTION | HEIGHT |
|---|---|---|
| 'Bravo' | Mellow red to orange-red | 2–3' |
| 'Fireball' | Rich red | 2–3' |
| 'Freckles' | Bright yellow with magenta spots | 2' |
| 'French Vanilla' | Soft creamy yellow | 2–3' |
| 'Haydee' | Buttercup yellow | 2–3' |

| CULTIVAR | DESCRIPTION | HEIGHT |
|---|---|---|
| 'Heritage' | Warm, mellow red with small spots | 2–3' |
| 'Matchless' | Rich orange-red | 2–3' |
| 'Melon Time' | Melon orange | 3–4' |
| 'Mont Blanc' | Pure white | 2–3' |
| 'Rosefire' | Orange-red bicolor | 3–4' |
| 'Utopia' | Bright buttercup yellow | 2–3' |
| 'Vanessa' | Bright yellow | 2–3' |
| 'Venture' | Intense burgundy red | 2–3' |
| 'Zephyr' | Clear rose-pink, spotted | 3–4' |

• **Hybrid Asiatic lilies:** Although these lilies grow taller than the other hybrids, the stems are quite strong and support the abundance of blooms, usually not requiring staking. They are early bloomers, from mid-June to July. The petals are turned back and many varieties are speckled. 'Enchantment,' which is a brilliant red-orange, is difficult to blend with other perennials. Again (as always, this is a highly subjective matter), select colors carefully so as to blend in with other plantings, as some are quite overwhelming.

| CULTIVAR | DESCRIPTION | HEIGHT |
|---|---|---|
| 'Connecticut King' | Large yellow flower with gold over-tones | 4' |
| 'Connecticut Yankee' | Apricot-orange with secondary buds that extend bloom | 4' |
| 'Enchantment' | 10 to 16 nasturtium red blooms per plant | 3' |
| 'Gypsy' | Candy pink star-shaped flowers with carmine spots and yellow throat | 4' |
| 'Prominence' | Glowing cherry red | 2½–3' |
| 'Sterling Star' | Ivory star-shaped flowers with wine-colored spots | 4–5' |

*Since 'Enchantment,' a hybrid Asiatic lily, is so brilliantly colored, it should be used in moderation in a border.*

• *Speciosum* **lilies:** Many consider these the most beautiful of all the lilies. Certainly the *L. speciosum* var. *rubrum* is one of the most popular of all lilies and is even available in florist shops. Although they can grow to a height of four or even five feet, they rarely need staking. There are many varieties available, with more being introduced each year. They are rarely available at garden centers and nurseries, so order them early from mail-order bulb suppliers, as these are the first of the lilies they run out of. They bloom from late July through August.

| CULTIVAR | DESCRIPTION | HEIGHT |
|---|---|---|
| 'Album' | Pure white—new and expensive but a showstopper | 3–4' |
| 'Bi-Centennial' | Glowing rose with white edges | 3–4' |

| CULTIVAR | DESCRIPTION | HEIGHT |
|---|---|---|
| 'Star Gazer' | Deep pink with dark red spots and bright white petal edges, a dwarf variety | 1½' |
| 'Uchida' | The best known of this species, it possesses large, graceful flowers of rich pink shading to brilliant crimson at the center of the petal and dark red spots all over | 4–5' |

• There are a number of other lilies available (some of which are listed below) that are classified as **"true species of lilies"** by the Royal Horticultural Society in Great Britain and by the North American Lily Society.

• **Tiger lilies** (*L. lancifolium*, syn. *tigrinum*): Most of these cultivars are spotted, with the petals turned back. They bloom from late July to September, filling a gap in garden color. Each produces from twelve to twenty flowers per stem. They reach a height of three to four feet. Here again, be careful in your color selection—some varieties tend to be garish.

| CULTIVAR | DESCRIPTION | HEIGHT |
|---|---|---|
| *L. l. fortunei* | Large, gleaming salmon-orange with black dots | 3–4' |
| *L. l. rose* | Lovely rich pink with black dots | 3–4' |
| 'Red Fox' | Intense red, with black dots and a satin sheen | 3–4' |
| 'Sunny Twinkle' | Bright, shining yellow-gold with black dots | 3–4' |

| SPECIES | DESCRIPTION | BLOOM TIME | HEIGHT |
|---|---|---|---|
| *L. auratum* (Gold-band lily) | 10- to 12-inch yellow-banded white flowers | Late July/early August | 5–6' |
| *L. canadense* (Meadow lily) | 2- to 3-inch yellow, purple-brown spotted flowers | Late June/July | 2–5' |
| *L. candidum* (Madonna lily) | 3- to 4-inch white flowers | Late June/July | 2–6' |
| *L. chalcedonicum* (Scarlet Turk's cap lily) | 2- to 3-inch bright red flowers | July | 2–4' |
| *L. longiflorum* (Easter lily) | 6- to 8-inch white trumpet-shaped flowers | July | 2–3' |
| *L. martagon* (Turk's cap lily) | 2- to 3-inch pink flowers | June/July | 3–6' |
| *L. philadelphicum* (Wood lily) | 3- to 4-inch purple-spotted orange-red flowers | Late June/July | 1–3' |
| *L. superbum* (American Turk's cap lily) | 3- to 4-inch brown-spotted orange-scarlet flowers | Late July/early September | 3–8' |

| CULTIVAR | DESCRIPTION | HEIGHT |
|---|---|---|
| 'Torino' | Delicate cream-white with a hint of yellow and wine-red dots | 3–4' |
| 'White Tiger' | Pure white with maroon dots and stamens | 3–4' |
| 'Yellow Star' | Bright, buttery yellow with black dots | 3–4' |

*Bloom time:* Midsummer.
*Propagation:* In fall, after leaves yellow, dig up clumps and separate smaller bulbs that have formed around the larger bulbs. In zones 7 to 11, replant immediately. Elsewhere, winter over as directed under "Winter Care."
*Rodent-proof:* Yes.
*Winter care:* In zones 7 to 11, winter over in ground. Elsewhere—dig up in the fall after leaves yellow. Shake off the soil and dry for several days in an airy, shady, frost-free place. Store in dry sphagnum peat moss, perlite, or vermiculite at 50° to 65° F.

## *Ornithogalum thrysoides*
### CHINCHERINCHEE

These are related to the spring-blooming Star-of-Bethlehem. The flowers are particularly long-lasting.

*Type of bulb:* True bulb.
*Color:* White or yellow.
*Description:* 2-inch blossom clusters held over medium green straplike foliage.
*Height:* 6 to 8 inches.
*USDA zones:* 7 to 11—hardy; 6 and north—dig up in fall and store as directed under "Winter Care."
*Soil:* Average.
*Light:* Full sun or partial shade.
*Moisture:* Water during prolonged summer drought.
*Time to plant outdoors:* Spring, after all danger of frost has passed.
*Planting depth:* 3 inches.
*Spacing:* 3 to 4 inches apart.
*Care during growing season:* Scratch a light dusting of 9-9-6 fertilizer into the soil one month after leaves have emerged.

## *Oxalis deppei, and O. regnelli*
### IRON CROSS OXALIS; BRAZILIAN OXALIS

Grown outdoors, oxalis are not at all spectacular; however, they provide an easily grown, green ground cover in sunny and shady parts of the garden.

*Type of bulb:* Rhizome.
*Color:* Pink, red, or white.
*Description:* 1-inch blossoms held over tidy mounds of shamrocklike foliage.
*Height:* 4 to 8 inches.
*USDA zones:* 8 to 11—hardy; 7 and north—dig up in the fall and store as directed under "Winter Care."
*Soil:* Ordinary, enriched with sphagnum peat moss and well-rotted compost or manure.
*Light:* Full sun or light shade.
*Moisture:* Water during prolonged periods of drought.
*Time to plant outdoors:* Spring, after all danger of frost has passed.
*Planting depth:* 2 inches.
*Spacing:* 4 inches apart.
*Care during growing season:* Scratch a light dust-

Oxalis regnelli *is an easy-to-grow tender bulb, ideal for providing dashes of white and shamrock-shaped foliage to a shade garden.*

ing of 9-9-6 fertilizer into the soil when leaves emerge.

*Bloom time:* Continuously from early summer through fall.

*Propagation:* When you dig up the plants in the fall, separate the masses of small rhizomes that have developed around the large ones. Save them all, as even the smallest will produce flowering plants the following year.

*Rodent-proof:* Yes.

*Winter care:* In zones 8 to 11, winter over in ground. Elsewhere, dig up after first light frost. Brush off soil. Dry in an airy, shady, frost-free place until leaves wither, then remove the leaves and store in a nylon stocking or mesh onion bag at 50° to 70° F.

## Polianthes tuberosa
### TUBEROSE

Back in the days when flowers were de rigueur at all funerals, the tuberose became associated with sad occasions, and so were rarely grown in gardens. Today, however, they have lost that stigma and are once again finding favor with gardeners who wish to plant highly scented gardens. Consider planting these splendidly fragrant flowers near a terrace or window so you can enjoy the lovely scent.

*Type of bulb:* Rhizome.
*Color:* White.
*Description:* 2-inch, single or double blossoms on 15-inch to 4-foot tall stems with medium green straplike foliage.
*Height:* 15 inches to 4 feet, depending on variety.
*USDA zones:* Although hardy in 9 to 11, it is best to dig them up in all zones in the fall and winter over indoors as directed in "Winter Care."
*Soil:* Ordinary, enriched with sphagnum peat moss and well-rotted compost or manure.
*Light:* Full sun.
*Moisture:* Water regularly during prolonged summer drought.
*Time to plant outdoors:* Spring, after all danger of frost has passed.
*Planting depth:* 3 inches.
*Spacing:* 6 to 8 inches apart.
*Care during growing season:* Scratch a light dusting of 9-9-6 fertilizer into the soil a month after the leaves emerge and every 4 weeks thereafter.

The old-fashioned tuberose (Polianthes tubero-sa), *if planted near a patio or porch, will scent the air during late summer and early fall.*

*Bloom time:* Mid- to late summer.

*Length of bloom:* 4 weeks.

*Propagation:* In late fall, before the first frost, dig up clumps and separate the smaller bulbs that have formed around the larger bulbs. In zones 8 to 11, replant immediately. Elsewhere, winter over as directed in "Winter Care."

*Rodent-proof:* Yes.

*Winter care:* In all zones, dig up in fall after tops turn brown, cut stems off close to bulbs, and let dry in a warm, airy place for 2 weeks. Store in dry peat moss, perlite, or vermiculite at 55° to 65° F.

## *Ranunculus asiaticus*

PERSIAN BUTTERCUP, FRENCH BUTTERCUP, DUTCH BUTTERCUP, SCOTCH BUTTERCUP, TURBAN BUTTERCUP, DOUBLE BUTTERCUP

Ranunculuses are difficult to grow in the garden because they flower best in soil that is dry around the crown of the plant but moist under the roots. However, because each plant produces over seventy-five lovely flowers during the growing season, you might want to attempt container growing and thus try to satisfy these conditions. Special growing instructions appear below.

*Type of bulb:* Tuberous root.

*Color:* All colors except green and blue. Many combinations of yellow, orange, pink, red, and white.

*Description:* 2- to 5-inch single or double blossoms on stalks held over fernlike foliage.

*Height:* 18 inches.

*USDA zones:* 8 to 11—hardy, but it is recommended that you dig up after foliage withers and store; 7 and north—dig up after foliage withers and store as directed under "Winter Care."

*Soil:* Well-drained, sandy loam.

*Light:* Full sun.

*Moisture:* Water regularly during prolonged summer drought only.

*Planting instructions:* In spring, after all danger of frost has passed, soak the tubers in water for 3 or 4 hours before planting. Remove the bottoms of clay pots and set them into the garden with their rims 1½ inches above the soil line. Fill the pot to within 3 inches of its rim with sandy loam. Place several tubers, claw side down, on top and cover with 1½ inches of loam. Water thoroughly and don't water again until shoots appear, unless the soil becomes very dry. Protect from birds, which relish the shoots, by covering the tops of the pots with cheesecloth until the shoots are about 4 inches high.

*Bloom time:* From mid- to late summer.
*Length of bloom:* 2 months of successive bloom.
*Propagation:* Divide tubers after foliage wilts.
*Rodent-proof:* Yes.
*Winter care:* In all zones, dig up the bulbs after the foliage withers, brush off the soil, and store at 50° to 55° F in dry peat moss, perlite, or vermiculite.

## Sparaxis
HARLEQUIN FLOWER, WANDFLOWER

Harlequin flowers grow best in the American West and Southwest, where the soil dries out in the summer. If you wish to grow them in other parts of the country, it is best to plant them in containers and treat them as houseplants; in that way you can provide the very dry summer conditions necessary for their survival. There are, however, many other bulbs suitable for containers that are easier to grow and will provide a more gratifying display of flowers. The foliage will yellow, then disappear in summer.

*Type of bulb:* Corm.
*Color:* Red, yellow, blue, purple, mauve, or white blossoms with bright yellow and black throats.
*Description:* 2-inch star-shaped blossoms on spikes held over sword-shaped foliage.
*Height:* 12 to 18 inches.
*USDA zones:* 9 to 11—hardy; 8 and north—bring potted bulbs indoors in the fall and store as directed under "Winter Care."

*Soil:* Well drained, ordinary.
*Light:* Full sun.
*Moisture:* Requires average moisture in spring but very dry soil in summer.
*Time to plant or bring potted bulbs outdoors:* Spring, after all danger of frost has passed.
*Planting depth:* 2 to 3 inches.
*Spacing:* 2 to 3 inches apart.
*Care during growing season:* Provide dry conditions during summer after bloom.
*Bloom time:* Late spring/early summer—depending on zone.
*Length of bloom:* 1 week.
*Propagation:* In the fall, unpot and remove small corms that have developed beside the original corms. Replant in pots and start anew.
*Rodent-proof:* Yes.
*Winter care:* In zones 9 to 11, winter over in ground. Elsewhere, before first frost, bring pots indoors, withhold water, and allow plant to go dormant. Store at room temperature out of direct sun. In early spring, resume watering and fertilize with any houseplant fertilizer according to instructions on label.

## Tigridia pavonia
TIGERFLOWER, MEXICAN SHELLFLOWER

Tigridias are very easy to grow and their interesting color combinations add an exotic touch to any garden.

*Type of bulb:* True bulb.
*Color:* White, yellow, orange, scarlet, pink, lilac, or buff.
*Description:* 5- to 6-inch blossoms on stems held over slightly untidy spearlike foliage.

*Bizarre, brilliant scarlet tigerflower* (Tigridia pavonia), *interplanted with soft pink cactus-flowering dahlias, provides a color contrast that will never be overlooked.*

*Height:* 18 to 30 inches.

*USDA zones:* 8 to 11—hardy; 7 and north—dig up in the fall and store as directed under "Winter Care."

*Soil:* Ordinary.

*Light:* Full sun or partial shade.

*Moisture:* Prefers moist conditions, so water regularly during entire season and particularly during prolonged summer drought.

*Time to plant outdoors:* Spring, after all danger of frost has passed.

*Planting depth:* 4 inches.

*Spacing:* 4 to 6 inches apart.

*Care during growing season:* Scratch a light dusting of 9-9-6 fertilizer into the soil once a month.

*Bloom time:* Mid- to late summer.

*Length of bloom:* Each flower blooms for only one day; however, each stem produces 6 to 10 flowers during the course of the summer.

*Propagation:* In the fall, separate the small bulbs that have formed around the larger ones and store as directed under "Winter Care."

*Rodent-proof:* Yes.

*Winter care:* In zones 8 to 11, winter over in ground. Elsewhere, dig up in the fall after leaves yellow. Shake off the soil and dry for several days in an airy, shady, frost-free place. Store in dry sphagnum peat moss, perlite, or vermiculite at 50° to 55° F.

# *Zantedeschia*
### CALLA LILY

The large, lovely calla lilies are best suited for growing in bogs or water gardens. However, the far smaller varieties are suitable for growing in the average garden. They are easily grown and stored over the winter and will certainly be a conversation piece in your garden.

*Type of bulb:* Rhizome.
*Color:* Pink, yellow, or white.
*Description:* Soft cone-shaped blossoms held over deep green, glossy foliage.
*Height:* From 1½ to 4 feet, depending on variety.
*USDA zones:* 8 to 11—hardy; 7 and north—dig up in the fall and store as directed under "Winter Care."
*Soil:* Ordinary, enriched with sphagnum peat moss and well-rotted compost or manure.
*Light:* Full sun with partial shade at midday or light shade.
*Moisture:* Keep well watered during prolonged summer drought.
*Time to plant outdoors:* Spring, after all danger of frost has passed.
*Planting depth:* 3 to 4 inches.
*Spacing:* 6 inches apart.
*Care during growing season:* Scratch a light dusting of 9-9-6 fertilizer into the soil once a month.
*Bloom time:* Early to late summer.
*Length of bloom:* 1 to 2 months.

*This yellow calla lily,* Zantedeschia elliottiana, *adds a dramatic touch to any garden.*

*Propagation:* Divide rhizomes in late summer or early fall after digging up or in the spring before planting.
*Rodent-proof:* Yes.
*Winter care:* In zones 8 to 11, winter over in ground. Elsewhere, dig up before the first frost, clean, and store in dry peat moss, perlite, or vermiculite at 40° to 50° F. If planted in pots, simply bring pot indoors, withhold water all winter, and store at 40° to 50° F. In the spring, after all danger of frost has

*Although it is difficult to grow, the classic white calla lily* (Zantedeschia aethiopica) *is so very beautiful, it is worth all of the extra effort and expertise involved.*

passed, water thoroughly and place out-doors.

## Recommended Zantedeschia

| SPECIES | COLOR | HEIGHT |
| --- | --- | --- |
| *Z. aethiopica* | White | 2–4' |
| *Z. a.* 'Crowborough' | White | 2½' |
| *Z. a. minor* | White | 2½' |
| *Z. elliottiana* | Yellow | 15–18" |
| *Z. rehmannii* | Pink | 15–18" |

*The delicate pink blossoms of low-growing fairy lilies (Zephyranthes) make them ideal plants for the front of a perennial border.*

## Zephyranthes
### FAIRY LILY, ZEPHYR LILY, RAIN LILY

Easily grown, these small pink lilies are particularly effective in a rock garden.

*Type of bulb:* True bulb.
*Color:* White and pink, yellow, rose, pink, apricot, or salmon, depending on variety.
*Description:* 2- to 5-inch lily-shaped blossoms on stems held over needlelike foliage.
*Height:* 6 to 8 inches.
*USDA zones:* 7 to 11—hardy; 6 and north—dig up in the fall and store as directed under "Winter Care."
*Soil:* Ordinary, enriched with sphagnum peat moss and well-rotted compost or manure.
*Light:* Full sun.
*Moisture:* Water regularly during prolonged summer drought.
*Time to plant outdoors:* Spring, after all danger of frost has passed.

*Planting depth:* 1 to 2 inches.
*Spacing:* 3 inches apart.
*Care during growing season:* None.
*Bloom time:* Mid- to late summer and fall, depending on variety.
*Length of bloom:* 1 week.
*Propagation:* After digging up in the fall, separate small bulbs that have developed around the larger ones and store as directed under "Winter Care."
*Rodent-proof:* Yes.
*Winter care:* In zones 7 to 11, winter over in ground. Elsewhere, dig up in the fall, allow to dry in an airy, shady, frost-free place, remove soil, and store in dry peat moss, perlite, or vermiculite at 50° to 60° F.

# Chapter Six

# BLOOMING BULBS

# FOR FALL

Just when you think the summer bulb season is over and the spectacular dahlias, lilies, fragrant tuberose, acidanthera, and others have staged their show, up pop the captivating little autumn crocuses, colchicums, and species cyclamens, as well as the stately lilylike blooms of lycoris, adding their color to the carpet of brilliant autumn leaves that have fallen to the ground. To the uninitiated, the sight of crocus blooming in the fall can be somewhat unnerving, since they are almost always thought of as being spring-blooming bulbs; to the bulb enthusiast, however, it is a sight that gladdens the heart. Crocuses are among the first bulbs to bloom in spring, and it seems fitting that there are varieties that are the last to bloom before winter. The following flowers will bring the outdoor bulb-growing season to a close in style.

## Colchicum
### AUTUMN CROCUS, MEADOW SAFFRON

Emerging out of the bare ground in early fall, colchicums extend the bulb season with their surprising crocuslike blooms. Most garden centers and nurseries offer only *Colchicum autumnale* (autumn crocus), with its pinkish white blossoms; however, mail-order sources often offer a lilac-and-white cultivar, 'Giant,' and 'Waterlily,' with double violet blooms. Since its foliage, which is not very attractive, emerges in spring, it is best to plant colchicums among shrubs where the foliage will not be on display.

*Type of bulb:* Corm.
*Color:* Lavender, violet, pink, white, or yellow (a spring bloomer).
*Description:* 2- to 4-inch chalice or star-shaped blossoms with undistinguished straplike prostrate foliage that emerges in spring and

*The pale purple color of the 'Double Waterlily' colchicum is a welcome sight in the early autumn garden.*

dries by late summer. Blossoms emerge from bare ground in early fall.

*Height:* 6 to 8 inches, depending on species.

*USDA zones:* 4 to 11.

*Soil:* Well drained, ordinary.

*Light:* Prefers full sun.

*Moisture:* Keep well watered during spring foliage growing season, water sparingly during midsummer dormancy, and resume regular watering when blossoms begin to emerge from soil in fall.

*Time to plant:* August (will bloom that fall).

*Planting depth:* 3 to 4 inches.

*Spacing:* 6 to 9 inches apart.

*Care during growing season:* Do not remove foliage until completely withered and brown. Scratch any kind of garden fertilizer into the soil around plants in the spring after shoots emerge.

*Bloom time:* Late summer/early fall.

*Length of bloom:* 2 to 3 weeks.

*Propagation:* Plantings may become crowded after 3 or 4 years. If so, after foliage withers in midsummer, dig up the corm clumps, separate the individual corms, remove the small corms that have formed around the larger ones, and replant all of them.

*Rodent-proof:* No.

*Naturalizing:* Yes, particularly along paths or walkways where they won't be hidden by taller-growing plants.

*Endangered species in the wild:* No.

## Recommended Colchicums

| SPECIES | COLOR | HEIGHT |
|---|---|---|
| C. autumnale | 2-inch pale rose to white flowers | 8″ |
| C. a. minor | 2-inch pale rose to white flowers | 6″ |
| C. byzantinum | 4-inch rose-lilac flowers | 6″ |
| C. luteum* | 2-inch bright yellow flowers | 6″ |
| C. speciosum | 6- to 8-inch lavender or white flowers | 8–12″ |
| C. 'Waterlily' | 4- to 6-inch many-petaled pink flowers | 6″ |

\* *The only colchicum that blooms in spring rather than fall.*

## *Crocus* (Autumn Blooming)

Although crocuses are a traditional sign of spring, there are some species that bloom in the fall, even into the winter in milder areas. These are never available at local garden centers or nurseries; they must be ordered from mail-order houses.

*Type of bulb:* Corm.

*Color:* Lilac, white, purple, blue, or rose-lilac with white throat.

*Description:* 1-inch goblet-shaped blossoms on stems that are held over medium green grass-like foliage.

*Height:* 4 to 6 inches.

*USDA zones:* 3 to 11.

*Soil:* Well drained, ordinary, fortified with sphagnum peat moss and well-rotted compost or manure.

*Light:* Full sun or partial shade.

*Moisture:* Water throughout the season, especially during prolonged summer drought.

*Time to plant:* Spring or late summer for fall bloom.

*Planting depth:* 2 to 4 inches.

*Spacing:* 2 to 3 inches apart.

*Care during growing season:* Do not remove foliage until completely withered and brown.

*Crocuses in October! Yes, there are autumn-blooming species available for you to plant. Pictured here is* Crocus sativus.

Each year, when shoots emerge, scratch in one tablespoon of 9-9-6 fertilizer per square foot of planting area.

*Bloom time:* Fall/early winter.

*Length of bloom:* 2 weeks.

*Propagation:* Plantings may become crowded after 3 or 4 years. If so, after foliage withers in fall, dig up corm clumps, separate individual corms, remove the small corms that have formed around the larger ones, and replant all of them.

*Rodent-proof:* No.

*Naturalizing:* Yes.

*Endangered species in the wild:* No.

## Recommended Autumn-Blooming Crocus

| SPECIES | COLOR |
| --- | --- |
| C. cancellatus (Cross-barred crocus) | Lilac or white |
| C. longiflorus (Long-flower crocus) | Bright lilac |
| C. medius (Intermediate crocus) | Bright lilac |
| C. pulchellus | Bright lilac |
| C. sativus (Saffron crocus) | Lilac or white |
| C. speciosus (Showy crocus) | Lilac, purple, or blue |
| C. zonatus (Banded crocus) | Rose-lilac with white throat |

*Here, a planting of* Crocus zonatus *is naturalized in a woodland setting.*

## Cyclamen (Species)

These charming plants are miniature cousins of the popular, greenhouse-grown, large-flowering varieties available at florists and garden centers throughout the year. They are easily grown, but because they are so small, it is best to plant them where they can be viewed most easily. Since the foliage of many species does not emerge until late summer, be sure to place a marker over the planting so you don't dig up the area by mistake.

*Type of bulb:* Tuber.
*Color:* Shades of pink or white.
*Description:* ¾- to 1-inch butterflylike blossoms held over rosettes of heart-shaped or rounded foliage that is marbled or patterned in silver-white or light green.
*Height:* 4 to 5 inches.
*USDA zones:* 5 to 9. Zones 10 and 11 are too hot and zone 4 is usually too cold.
*Soil:* Well drained, sandy, enriched with sphagnum peat moss and well-rotted compost or manure.
*Light:* Prefers light shade.
*Moisture:* Keep well watered once foliage emerges; do not water once foliage begins to yellow.
*Time to plant:* Midsummer
*Planting depth:* Cover *neapolitanum* cyclamens with 2 inches of soil. All others should be set just beneath the soil.
*Spacing:* 6 to 8 inches apart.
*Care during growing season:* Each spring apply a light mulch of compost for nourishment. Scratch any kind of garden fertilizer into the soil after shoots emerge. Do not remove foliage until completely withered and brown.
*Bloom time:* Late summer and on into fall, depending on species.

*Length of bloom:* 1 to 2 weeks, depending on species.
*Propagation:* If you want more, purchase additional tubers. Propagation is best left to the experts.
*Rodent-proof:* Yes.
*Naturalizing:* No.
*Endangered species in the wild:* Yes; however, some have been propagated commercially. As of 1990, all cyclamens gathered in the wild and offered by Netherlands bulb growers will bear labels stating "Bulbs from Wild Source." Those unmarked are grown from cultivated stock. As of 1992, labels will state place of origin and be marked "Bulbs Grown from Cultivated Stock" or "Bulbs from Wild Source." See page 143 for more information.

## Recommended Species Cyclamen

| SPECIES | COLOR |
|---|---|
| C. cilicium | Pale rose |
| C. europaeum | Crimson-rose |
| C. neapolitanum | Rose or white |

## Lycoris
### SPIDER LILY

Lycoris, like some other autumn-blooming bulbs, sends up its foliage in spring and then goes into dormancy during summer, only to bloom in fall.

*Type of bulb:* True bulb.
*Color:* Red, pink, yellow, or white.
*Description:* Large, spiderlike blossoms on stalks. Straplike foliage appears in spring, then disappears. Flower stalks then emerge without foliage.

*Height:* 1½ to 2 feet.

*USDA zones:* 5 to 11, depending on species.

*Soil:* Well-drained, sandy, enriched with sphagnum peat moss and well-rotted compost or manure.

*Light:* Full sun or light shade.

*Moisture:* Water during spring foliage season. When foliage withers and dies, stop watering. When flower stalks appear, in late summer or fall, resume watering.

*Time to plant:* Midsummer for fall bloom.

*Planting depth:* Top of bulb neck should sit just beneath soil surface.

*Spacing:* 5 to 8 inches apart.

*Care during growing season:* Scratch any kind of garden fertilizer into soil around plants in spring after foliage emerges and in late summer when flower stalks emerge. Do not remove foliage until completely withered and brown.

*Bloom time:* Late summer/fall.

*Length of bloom:* 2 to 3 weeks.

*Propagation:* After foliage yellows, dig up bulbs and remove small ones that have formed around the larger ones. Replant immediately. Some species develop bulbs on top of faded flowers; simply remove them and plant immediately in nursery. It takes 3 years of growth for them to flower.

*Rodent-proof:* Yes.

*Naturalizing:* No.

*Endangered species in the wild:* No.

## Hardiest Lycoris Species

| SPECIES | COLOR | ZONES |
| --- | --- | --- |
| *L. aurea* (Golden spider lily) | Yellow | 8–11 |
| *L. radiata* (Red spider lily) | Red | 7–11 |
| *L. squamigera* (Magic lily) | Rose-lilac or pink (fragrant) | 5–11 |

## Sternbergia lutea

This charming yellow-flowering plant, bearing a resemblance to the spring yellow crocus, is no longer being offered by reputable bulb suppliers because it is an endangered species in the wild. At a future date, if they are propagated commercially, they will again become available. As of now, they are not available grown from cultivated stock.

If you have gardener friends who have a planting of sternbergia, prevail upon them for a few bulbs. Their bright yellow color is lovely amid the fallen leaves of autumn.

*Type of bulb:* True bulb.

*Color:* Yellow.

*Description:* 2-inch crocuslike blossoms, over 6- to 12-inch grasslike foliage.

*Height:* 4 inches.

*USDA zones:* 6 to 11.

*Soil:* Well drained, ordinary.

*Light:* Full sun.

*Moisture:* Prefers dry conditions. If plant does not thrive, it is usually because there is too much summer moisture. Move to a site with better drainage.

*Time to plant:* Midsummer for fall bloom.

*Planting depth:* 5 inches.

*The brilliant yellow of fall-blooming sternbergia adds sparkle to a bed of multicolored autumn leaves.*

*Spacing:* 3 inches apart.

*Care during growing season:* None. It is not necessary to fertilize sternbergia.

*Bloom time:* Early fall.

*Length of bloom:* 2 to 4 weeks.

*Propagation:* If planting becomes crowded, dig up in midsummer, separate bulbs, and replant immediately.

*Rodent-proof:* No.

*Naturalizing:* Yes.

*Endangered species in the wild:* Yes.

*In recent years, Hippeastrum, or amaryllis, has become a very popular Christmas plant. Here a group of them add a festive touch to the holiday mood.*

*Chapter Seven*

# FLOWERING BULBS
# FOR INDOORS

Even though the snow is on the ground and chilling winds whip through your garden, you can still enjoy the glorious beauty of bulbs inside your house. Many unusual bulbs that are not suitable for outdoor planting in most parts of the country, such as amaryllis and freesia, are perfectly adapted to indoor living, and others, such as spring-blooming daffodils, tulips, and hyacinths, can be "forced" into bloom indoors. Some bloom during the winter, others in early spring. At any rate, just because it's cold and damp outside, you needn't put aside the pleasure of growing bulbs.

Included in this chapter is some preliminary information on selecting containers, maintaining appropriate levels of humidity, pests and diseases particular to indoor-grown plants, and a special section on which bulbs to avoid, primarily because they are difficult to grow, followed by the "indoor" bulbs that are relatively easy to grow. Each entry includes specific information about

moisture requirements, planting medium, temperature requirements, and any special care required. Forcing is covered in Chapter 8.

## WHERE AND WHEN TO BUY
## YOUR BULBS

If you glance through the individual bulb entries that follow, you will note that some bulbs are best purchased at flower shops while in bloom. Others can be bought or ordered from local garden centers or nurseries, or through mail-order sources (see pages 144–45).

Usually, such bulbs as amaryllis can be purchased locally toward the end of the fall, in time for Christmas blooming.

## DIFFICULT BULBS AND THOSE NOT READILY AVAILABLE

There is a large number of flowering bulbs that are either not readily available or, if they are, are very difficult to bring to flower by the average plant enthusiast. Sometimes you find these bulbs offered in mail-order catalogues, but the suppliers rarely let you know about the problems you might encounter. Below is a list of a few, included so that you can avoid the inevitable frustration of either not being able to locate them or not being able to bring them to flowering.

• *Cypella*—Available only in seed form in this country, this plant takes about three years to come to flower.

• *Eucharis* (Amazon lily)—This lively bridal bouquet favorite can be grown as a houseplant; however, it requires very high humidity, often impossible to attain in a normal household environment. It is best to buy mature plants at a florist, if they are available, and to dispose of them after bloom.

• *Haemanthus* (Blood lily)—Very high humidity and bottom heat are required to bring blood lilies to bloom, a task best left to professional growers.

• *Milla* (Mexican star lily)—Available only in seed form in this country, this plant takes about three years to come to flower.

• *Moraea* (Peacock iris, Fortnight lily, Butterfly iris)—Available only in seed form in this country, this plant takes about three years to come to flower.

• *Nerine* (Guernsey lily)—Difficult to find

and difficult to grow. It is best to purchase a mature plant at a florist and dispose of it after flowering.

• *Pancratium* (Corsican lily, Spirit lily, Sea daffodil, Sea lily)—Difficult to find and difficult to grow.

• *Schizostylis* (Crimson flag)—Difficult to find and difficult to grow.

## INCREASING HUMIDITY

Some winter-blooming bulb plants require a high level of humidity. During the winter heating season, almost all homes suffer from very dry air conditions. There are many ways you can raise the humidity level around your plants. Here are some of them:

• *Grouping.* The moisture evaporating from a group of plants will raise the humidity level and create a miniature microclimate.

• *Water.* Place trays of water on nearby radiators. As the water evaporates the humidity level will rise.

• *Trays and pebbles.* Place plants on trays or deep saucers filled with a layer of pebbles or stones. Pour water into the tray to the level of the stones. Make sure your plants aren't sitting in water.

• *Glass and marbles.* Put colorful marbles in glass containers and fill the containers with water. Not only does this raise the humidity level, it's also quite attractive.

• *Colored bottles.* Fill a collection of colored bottles with water and intersperse them among your plants.

• *Misting.* Purchase inexpensive misters at garden centers or nurseries and spray foliage daily.

• *Washing foliage.* Not only does this raise the humidity level, it also helps keep plants clean, thus reducing pest and disease infestation. Use clean, lukewarm water and wash gently with a soft sponge once every two weeks.

• *Humidifiers.* This is probably the most effective way to raise the humidity level in a dry winter house, and not only is it good for your plants, it's good for you, too.

# CONTAINERS FOR INDOOR BULBS

Any number of containers are appropriate for growing flowering bulbs. With the exception of *Narcissus tazetta*, all require containers that have drainage holes in the bottom. Specific needs are indicated in each entry. If you decide upon a new or used clay or terra-cotta container, it must be treated before planting. Used plastic containers must also be treated before planting.

• *Brand new terra-cotta or clay container:* Soak overnight in water. This conditions the container so that it will not absorb water from the planting medium.

• *Used terra-cotta or clay container:* Soak overnight in a solution of one part household bleach to three parts water. This kills any disease organisms that might be on the surface of the container.

• *Used plastic container:* Soak overnight in the bleach solution.

# PESTS AND DISEASES

Since almost all flowering bulb plants are resistant to pests and practically disease-free, it is highly unlikely that you will have to cope with these problems. Diseases such as crown rot, fungus leaf rot, or mildew will most probably not cause any problem. However, since winter-blooming bulb plants are treated as houseplants, pests that might already have taken hold in your existing collection may attack your flowering bulb plants. Here are the ones to watch out for:

• *Aphids.* Small gray or green insects that cling to the undersides of leaves and stems, they feed on plant juices, causing leaves to yellow. They spread very fast.
REMEDY: Swab foliage with soapy water or spray with an insecticide containing pyrethrum or rotenone.

• *Mealybugs.* These hide under leaves and resemble bits of cotton. They suck the juices from the plant and cause the foliage to turn pale or drop from the plant. Stunted growth will also result.
REMEDY: Using a cotton swab dipped in alcohol, remove the bugs; then wash the foliage with soapy water.

• *Mites.* These infinitesimal pests cannot be seen with the naked eye. The effects of their presence are curling leaves, withered buds or tips, and webs on the undersides of leaves.
REMEDY: Cut away and dispose of infected foliage, then spray with dicofol. However, if mites attack your florist cyclamen, the only thing to do is throw it out.

• *Red spider.* Their many cobwebs make foliage look dusty. Leaves will turn yellow and drop off.

REMEDY: Dip the plant in a solution of two teaspoons malathion to one gallon of water.

• *Thrips.* These tiny insects leave a white mottled look on leaves.

REMEDY: Spray with malathion according to manufacturer's instructions on label.

• *Whiteflies.* If plant is disturbed, adult whiteflies will rise like a cloud. Leaves turn pale or yellow and eventually drop off.

REMEDY: These are difficult to control. Spray once a week for one month with rotenone or malathion according to the manufacturer's instructions on the label.

## *Clivia*
### KAFFIR LILY

These Victorian favorites are making a big comeback these days because they burst forth with spectacular bloom during the doldrums of late winter and early spring. It is best to purchase plants in the fall or winter at a florist, garden center, or nursery. Although they are expensive, they are relatively easy to maintain and continue to bloom year after year.

*Type of bulb:* Tuberous root.
*Color:* Orange, yellow, salmon, scarlet, or white.
*Description:* Clusters of 12 to 20 fragrant blossoms, each 2 inches wide, held on stalks over straplike evergreen leaves that arch gracefully. Decorative red berries form after flowers have bloomed.
*Height:* 2 feet.
*USDA zones:* Hardy only in zones 9 to 11. However, because they prefer a pot-bound growing environment, they are usually grown in containers in these zones. Grow as house-

plants in all other zones.
*Soil:* To make 2 quarts of soil medium—enough to pot one bulb in an 8-inch pot—mix together ⅓ quart peat moss, ⅓ quart packaged potting soil, and 1⅓ quarts sharp sand.
*Light:* Semi-shade. No direct sunlight. An east- or west-facing window is best.
*Moisture:* After bloom, let dry out slightly between waterings. From late fall until midwinter, water only enough to keep leaves from wilting. Once flower buds set, water freely, but avoid stagnant water in pot.
*Humidity:* Normal home humidity is sufficient.
*Temperature:* Cool. It is *very* important during the fall of the second year, if you wish to bring the plant back to bloom, to maintain cool temperatures—from 40° to 50° F at night and 65° F or lower during the day—for entire flowering cycle.
*Fertilizing:* After buds have set in late midwinter, fertilize once a month with any liquid houseplant fertilizer at half the recommended strength. After bloom and until late fall, feed every 6 weeks at half the recommended strength. From late fall until the buds set, do not feed.
*Planting instructions:* Since plant prefers pot-bound growing conditions, select a clay container no more than 2 inches larger in diameter than the root mass. *Do not use a plastic container.* Prepare clay container as instructed on page 121. Place 1½ inches of drainage material in the bottom of the container. (You can use broken flowerpot shards, pebbles, or the plastic "popcorn" used by mail-order companies to ship goods.) Fill the bottom few inches of the pot with the planting medium. Set the bulb on the planting medium so that bulb tips are barely covered. Fill the rest of the pot with planting medium to within 1 inch of the top

*The classic, old-fashioned favorite, clivia, can be purchased in bloom at florist shops or as bare-root bulbs through mail-order sources.*

of the pot. Water thoroughly.

*Care during growing season:* Keep leaves dry and clean. If water collects at base of leaf cluster, use an absorbent paper towel to remove.

*Bloom time:* Mid- to late winter.

*Length of bloom:* 2 to 4 weeks, depending on growing conditions.

*Propagation:* After 3 or 4 years, it will be time to repot. Unpot plant when foliage has dried, remove the small plants that have formed at the base of the older plant, and replant. They will grow and may flower after 3 years.

## Crinum
### SWAMP CRINUM, FLORIDA CRINUM

This unusual flowering bulb can be grown indoors in the North. Its height, however, makes it look somewhat ungainly unless one has the proper setting for it. It blooms in summer and requires some care but is usually not at all problematical.

*Type of bulb:* True bulb.

*Color:* Rose, red, white, pink, or combinations thereof.

*Description:* Massive clusters of 3- to 6-inch lily-shaped blossoms on stiff stalks over green straplike foliage.

*Height:* 2 to 3 feet.

*USDA zones:* Hardy in zones 8 to 11. Treat as houseplants in all other zones.

*Soil:* To make 2 quarts of soil medium, enough to pot one bulb in a 6-inch pot, mix together 2/3 quart peat moss, 2/3 quart packaged potting soil, and 2/3 quart sharp sand or perlite. Add 1/2 teaspoon of ground limestone.

*Light:* Southern exposure—plant requires at least 4 hours of direct sun a day during growing season.

*An unusual winter-flowering bulb that is easily grown indoors is crinum, here pictured* Crinum x powellii.

*Moisture:* Keep moist throughout growing season, from April through September. After growing season, when foliage dies down and plant goes into dormant stage, let soil become slightly dry and water very sparingly. The following spring, when new growth begins, slowly increase moisture and resume care.

*Humidity:* There is no need to increase humidity.

*Temperature:* Cool. Prefers 50° to 60° F at night and 68° to 70° F during the daytime during dormant winter season.

*Fertilizing:* Feed monthly from April to December with any liquid houseplant fertilizer at half the recommended strength. Each year, early in the fall, hose away some of the surface planting medium, without exposing roots, and replace it with fresh planting medium.

*Time to plant:* Late winter.

*Planting instructions:* Since plant prefers potbound growing conditions, select a container no more than 2 inches larger in diameter than the bulb. Plant 1 bulb in a 6-inch pot or 3 bulbs in a 12-inch pot. Place 1 inch of drainage material in the bottom of the container. (You can use broken flowerpot shards, pebbles, or the plastic "popcorn" used by mail-order companies to ship goods.) Fill the bottom few inches of the pot with the planting medium. Set the bulb on the soil so its tips are barely covered. Fill the rest of the pot with the planting medium to within 1 inch of the top of the pot. Water thoroughly.

*Care during growing season:* Flowers more profusely when potbound, so do not repot until roots are very crowded, usually after 3 or 4 years. Make sure to repot after the foliage has withered. Remove faded flower petals and cut off entire blossom when it has turned yellow. Do not remove foliage until it turns brown.

*Bloom time:* Summer.

*Length of bloom:* 1 to 2 weeks.

*Propagation:* After 3 or 4 years, when it is time to repot, remove the offsets that have formed and replant. Offsets will grow and may flower after 3 years.

## Recommended Crinums

| SPECIES OR CULTIVAR | COLOR |
|---|---|
| C. americanum | White |
| C. asiaticum | White |
| C. bulbispermum (syn. C. capense) | Rose with white throat |
| C. 'Cecil Houdyshel' | Pink |
| C. 'Ellen Bousanquet' | Wine-red |
| C. moorei | White with red stripes |
| C. powellii | Reddish pink or white |

## *Cyclamen persicum* (Florist's)

Hybridizers have been busy creating an entire new generation of cyclamens, many of which are dwarf varieties that are compact and manageable as houseplants and come in a wider range of colors. Because of very specific growing requirements, it is best to purchase plants at your local florist, garden center, or nursery in the fall. However, once the plant has bloomed, it is easily brought to bloom year after year.

*Type of bulb:* Tuber.

*Color:* Pink, white, red, purple, or combinations thereof.

*Description:* 2- to 3-inch butterfly-shaped blossoms on stalks held over lush, attractive, variegated foliage.

*Height:* 12 to 18 inches, depending on variety.

*USDA zones:* Hardy only in zones 10 and 11. Treat as houseplants in all other zones.

*Soil:* To make 2 quarts of soil medium, enough to pot one tuber in an 8-inch pot, mix together ⅔ quart peat moss, ⅔ quart packaged potting soil, and ⅔ quart sharp sand or perlite. Add ½ teaspoon of ground limestone.

*Light:* Bright, indirect, or curtain-filtered sunlight.

*The soft pink of these cyclamen (Cyclamen persicum), available everywhere at florists and some nurseries, blends well with almost all interior colors.*

*Moisture:* Water at least once a week while in bloom, keeping evenly moist. Do not overwater. After bloom, water sparingly until all leaves have faded. Then withhold water for one month. Resume watering sparingly until plant is in bud, then begin weekly watering.

*Humidity:* Mist daily and raise humidity level.

*Temperature:* Cool during bloom period. Prefers 40° to 55° F at night and 65° F or lower during the daytime.

*Fertilizing:* During indoor growing season, feed once a week with any liquid houseplant fertilizer at ⅓ the recommended strength. In the garden, fertilize at half the recommended strength once a month.

*Growing instructions:* After the blooming cycle, remove the plant from the pot and plant outdoors in the garden in partial shade. In the fall, before the first frost, dig up the plant and repot, one tuber per 8-inch pot. Place 1 inch of drainage material in the bottom of the container. (You can use broken flowerpot shards, pebbles, or the plastic "popcorn" used by mail-order companies to ship goods.) Fill about ⅓ of the pot with the planting medium. Set the tuber on the planting medium so that ⅓ is above soil line. Fill the rest of the pot with the planting medium to within 1 inch of the top of the pot. Water thoroughly.

*Care during growing season:* Remove spent flowers and faded foliage during growing season.

*Bloom time:* Fall and winter.

*Length of bloom:* Continuous throughout fall and winter.

## Freesia

Unless treated with a growth retardant, freesia foliage and flower stems will grow very tall and rangy in the average house. Using the retardant is a complicated business, so it's not recommended for the houseplant enthusiast. If you don't mind the unattractive appearance of the foliage and stalks, you might want to try your hand at growing these wonderfully scented flowers. I have tried and was successful in getting some blooms.

*Type of bulb:* Corm.

*Color:* All colors of the rainbow.

*Although the foliage of freesia is quite rangy, their lovely scented blooms, which can perfume an entire room, make them desirable houseplants.*

*Description:* Highly fragrant, 2-inch blossoms along wiry stems that require support.

*Height:* 1 to 1½ feet.

*USDA zones:* Hardy only in zones 9 to 11. Treat as houseplants in all other zones.

*Soil:* To make 2 quarts of soil medium, enough to pot 12 bulbs in an 8-inch pot, mix together ⅔ quart peat moss, ⅔ quart packaged potting soil, and ⅔ quart sharp sand or perlite. Add ½ teaspoon of ground limestone.

*Light:* Keep in dim (not dark) location until growth starts to show. Then move to full sun (requires 4 hours direct sun a day).

*Moisture:* Once shoots appear, keep consistently moist until the foliage withers after bloom. Then withhold water until foliage dies.

*Humidity:* Normal winter indoor humidity is sufficient.

*Temperature:* Cool. Prefers 60° to 65° F at night and 70° F in the daytime during winter heating season.

*Fertilizing:* Feed monthly with any liquid houseplant fertilizer at half the recommended strength from the time shoots emerge until buds show color. Then discontinue feeding.

*Time to plant:* Early to late winter.

*Planting instructions:* Place 1 inch of drainage material in the bottom of the container. (You can use broken flowerpot shards, pebbles, or the plastic "popcorn" used by mail-order companies to ship goods.) Fill about ⅔ of the pot with the planting medium. Set bulbs so that the tops will be an inch below the soil, then fill the rest of the pot with planting medium to within 1 inch of the top of the pot. Water thoroughly.

*Care during growing season:* When growth reaches 4 to 5 inches, the grasslike leaves need support. Insert 4 bamboo sticks into the pot and tie green string around the legs at the level of the leaves. As the leaves grow, a second tying about 5 inches above the first is recommended. After bloom, cut off the faded blossoms. When the last blossom has faded, allow foliage to wither and brown naturally.

*Postbloom care:* After bloom, the corm must rest. Do not water or fertilize. When the leaves die, remove the corms from the pot and store in mesh bags or old nylon stockings in a dry place at room temperature until the following planting season.

*Bloom time:* About 6 weeks after starting bulb in fall or winter.

*Length of bloom:* 2 to 3 weeks.

*Propagation:* At end of growing season, when you remove corms from pots, separate small corms that develop beside large ones, and store. Plant in winter. It will take several years before these bloom. However, corms are so inexpensive that if you want more, it is best to simply purchase them.

## *Hippeastrum*
### AMARYLLIS

These spectacular flowering bulbs are among the easiest to bring to bloom, and each year lovelier varieties are offered at garden centers, at nurseries, and in mail-order catalogues. Dwarf versions have been introduced recently; although as of now, they are available only in scarlet, they are so popular that other varieties will soon be available. They are rapidly becoming a classic Christmas plant, with their varying shades of reds, pinks, and whites complementing holiday decor.

*Type of bulb:* True bulb.
*Color:* Red, pink, white, orange, scarlet, striped, or combinations thereof.
*Description:* 3 or 4 lily-shaped blossoms of 8 to 10 inches each held on erect stalks over medium green straplike foliage.
*Height:* 1 to 2 feet.
*USDA zones:* Hardy only in zones 9 to 11. Treat as houseplants in all other zones.
*Soil:* To make 2 quarts of soil medium, enough to pot 1 bulb in an 8-inch pot, mix together ⅔ quart peat moss, ⅔ quart packaged potting soil, and ⅔ quart sharp sand or perlite. Add ½ teaspoon of ground limestone.
*Light:* Southern exposure—requires at least 4 hours of direct sun a day during growing season.

*Also known as amaryllis, the very large, flamboyant blooms of* Hippeastrum *have become a Christmas favorite all over the world. Pictured here is the cultivar 'Midnight.'*

*Moisture:* Once stalk appears, keep plant moderately moist until leaves begin to yellow in late summer. It is a good idea to water very well when necessary and then wait until soil at the top of the pot is dusty and dry to water again. Reduce water at the end of the summer and withhold completely during rest period. Do this until you wish to start plant growing again.
*Humidity:* Normal winter indoor humidity is sufficient.

*Temperature:* Moderate. Prefers 60° to 65° F at night and 70° F or higher in the daytime during winter heating season.

*Fertilizing:* Feed monthly from time stalk emerges to dormant period with any liquid houseplant fertilizer, at half recommended strength. Do not fertilize during dormancy. Each year, before restarting bulbs, hose away some of the surface planting medium, without exposing the roots, and replace with fresh planting medium.

*Planting instructions:* Since plant prefers moderately potbound growing conditions, select a container 4 inches larger in diameter than the bulb. Plant a bulb in an 8-inch pot or 3 bulbs in a 12-inch pot. Place an inch of drainage material in the bottom of a container. (You can use broken flowerpot shards, pebbles, or the plastic "popcorn" used by mail-order companies to ship goods.) Fill the bottom few inches of the pot with planting medium. Set the bulb so that fully half of the bulb will be above the soil. Fill the rest of the pot with planting medium to within an inch of the top of the pot. Water thoroughly. Do not water again until stalk appears.

*Time to plant:* For Christmas bloom, start in October.

*Care during growing season:* Remove faded flower petals. When last blossom has faded, cut stalk about 5 inches above the point where it emerges from the bulb.

*Postbloom care:* After it has bloomed—usually about 2 months after planting—the bulb is exhausted. It is smaller, slightly soft, and must be rebuilt in order to bloom the following year. Allow leaves to grow at least 6 months. It is best to leave the bulb in the pot and care for it, rather than removing it and planting it in the garden, but you can sink the pot into the ground in the garden if you wish. During this rebuilding period, the bulb should produce from 7 to 11 leaves. At the end of August, slowly withdraw water until leaves wilt. This takes about 3 weeks. When yellow, cut the leaves off 3 inches above the neck. Remove the pot from the garden and rest the bulb in its pot for a month in a cool, dark place, then move to where a daytime temperature of 70° F is maintained for 3 weeks. Nighttime temperatures from 55° to 70° F are suitable. Do not water during this period. Average room light is sufficient. After this "curing" period, you can start the bulb growing. To delay starting, place in a cool place, about 45° to 55° F, and withhold water until ready.

*Bloom time:* About 6 weeks after starting bulb in fall or winter.

*Length of bloom:* 2 to 3 weeks.

*Propagation:* After 3 or 4 years, it will be time to repot. Unpot plant when foliage has dried, remove any offsets that have formed, and store bulb and offsets in dry peat moss in a shady, dry, warm place until ready to plant. Offsets may flower the second year.

## *Lachenalia*
CAPE COWSLIP, LEOPARD LILY

These charming plants are quite manageable in terms of size for a houseplant collection and are relatively easy to grow. Purchase the bulbs in August or September from mail-order sources—they're not usually available at nurseries or garden centers.

*Type of bulb:* True bulb.

*Color:* Yellow, orange, red, or coral.

*Description:* 6-inch spikes of 1-inch blossoms held on stalks over ribbonlike leaves that are often spotted with purple.

*Height:* 9 to 12 inches.

*USDA zones:* Hardy only in zones 9 to 11, but even there they are usually grown as houseplants. Treat as houseplants in all other zones.

*Soil:* To make 2 quarts of soil medium, enough to pot up 2 5-inch bulb pans, mix together ⅔ quart peat moss, ⅔ quart packaged potting soil, and ⅔ quart sharp sand or perlite. Add ½ teaspoon of ground limestone.

*Light:* Southern exposure—requires at least 4 hours of direct sun a day during growing season.

*Moisture:* Keep moist throughout growing season, from planting time in late summer throughout bloom period in winter. After growing season, when foliage dies down and plant goes into dormant stage, stop watering.

*Humidity:* Normal. There is no need to increase humidity.

*Temperature:* Very cool during growing season. Prefers 50° F or lower at night and normal house temperature during the day.

*Fertilizing:* Feed monthly during growing season with any liquid houseplant fertilizer at half recommended strength. Withhold fertilizer after the blooms fade.

*Time to plant:* Late summer/early fall.

*Planting instructions:* Select a 5-inch bulb pan for every 6 bulbs you wish to plant. Place an inch of drainage material in the bottom of the container. (You can use broken flowerpot shards, pebbles, or the plastic "popcorn" used by mail-order companies to ship goods.) Fill the bottom few inches of the pot with the planting medium. Set the bulb so bulb tips are just beneath the soil's surface. Fill the rest of the pot with planting medium to within an inch of the top of the pot. Water

thoroughly. Do not water again until shoots emerge from soil.

*Postbloom care:* Remove faded flower petals and cut off entire blossom when it has turned yellow. After bloom, when foliage has withered, remove bulbs from pot, clean, put in mesh bags or old nylon stocking, and store in shady, dry place until following fall.

*Bloom time:* Late winter/early spring.

*Length of bloom:* 1 to 2 weeks.

*Propagation:* When you unpot plant after bloom, remove small bulbs that have formed on the main bulb, store, and plant in the fall. It may take 2 to 3 years for these small bulbs to grow to blooming size, so it is better to purchase blooming-size bulbs if you want more.

## Recommended Lachenalia

| SPECIES | COLOR |
| --- | --- |
| L. aloides (syn. L. tricolor) | Green with red-and-yellow bands |
| L. a. lutea | Yellow |
| L. bulbifera (syn. L. pendula) | Purple, yellow, or coral combinations |

## Sprekelia formosissima
AZTEC LILY, JACOBEAN LILY, ST. JAMES LILY

These cousins of the popular amaryllis make a charming addition to any houseplant collection.

*Type of bulb:* True bulb.

*Color:* Bright red.

*Description:* 4-inch lily-shaped blossoms held on erect stalks over medium green straplike foliage.

*Height:* 12 to 18 inches.

*USDA zones:* Hardy in zones 8 to 11. Treat as houseplants in all other zones.

*Soil:* To make 2 quarts of soil medium, enough to pot 1 bulb in an 8-inch pot, mix together ⅔ quart peat moss, ⅔ quart packaged potting soil, and ⅔ quart sharp sand or perlite. Add ½ teaspoon of ground limestone.

*Light:* Southern exposure—requires at least 4 hours of direct sun a day during growing season.

*Moisture:* Once stalk appears, keep plant moderately moist until leaves begin to yellow in late summer. It is a good idea to water very well when necessary and then wait until soil at the top of the pot is dusty and dry before watering again. Reduce water at the end of the summer and withhold completely during rest period. Do this until about a month before you wish to start plant growing again.

*Humidity:* Normal winter indoor humidity is sufficient.

*Temperature:* Moderate. Prefers 60° to 65° F at night and 72° F or higher in the daytime during winter heating season.

*Fertilizing:* Feed monthly from time the stalk emerges to dormant period with any liquid houseplant fertilizer at half recommended strength. Each year, before restarting bulbs, hose away some of the surface planting medium, without exposing the roots, and replace with fresh soil mix.

*Time to plant:* Late fall/winter.

*Planting instructions:* Since plant prefers moderately potbound growing conditions, select a container 4 inches larger in diameter than the bulb. Plant one bulb in an 8-inch pot or 3 bulbs in a 12-inch pot. Place an inch of drainage material in the bottom of the container. (You can use broken flowerpot shards, pebbles, or the plastic "popcorn" used by mail-order companies to ship goods.) Fill the bottom few inches of the pot with planting medium. Set the bulb so fully half of the bulb will be above the soil. Fill the rest of the pot with planting medium to within an inch of the top of the pot. Water thoroughly once. Do not water again until stalk appears.

*Care during growing season:* Remove faded flower petals. When last blossom has faded, cut stalk about 5 inches above where it emerges from the bulb.

*Postbloom care:* After it has bloomed—usually about 2 months after planting—the bulb is exhausted. It is smaller, slightly soft, and must be rebuilt to bloom the following year. Allow leaves to grow for at least 6 months. It is best to leave the bulb in the pot and care for it, rather than placing it in the garden. During this rebuilding period, the bulb should produce from 7 to 11 leaves. At the end of August, slowly withdraw water until leaves wilt. This takes about 3 weeks. When yellow, cut the leaves off 3 inches above the neck. Rest the bulb in its pot for a month in a cool, dark place, then bring it into an area that maintains a 70° F temperature for three weeks. Do not water during this period. After this "curing" period, you can start bulb growing again. To delay start, place in a cool place, about 45° to 55° F, and withhold water until ready.

*Bloom time:* Winter/early spring, about 6 weeks after starting bulb.

*Length of bloom:* 2 to 3 weeks.

*Propagation:* After 3 or 4 years, it will be time to repot. Unpot plant when foliage has dried, remove offsets that have formed, and store bulb and offsets in dry peat moss in a shady, dry, warm place until ready to plant. Offsets may flower the second year.

## Vallota speciosa
### SCARBOROUGH LILY

These spectacular blooming bulbous plants are particularly well suited to indoor cultivation by the average houseplant enthusiast.

*Type of bulb:* True bulb.

*Color:* Brilliant red-orange; occasionally, pink or white varieties are available.

*Description:* Clusters of 3 to 10 trumpet-shaped blossoms—3 to 4 inches each—held on stiff stalks over green straplike foliage.

*Height:* 2 feet.

*USDA zones:* Hardy only in zones 10 and 11. Treat as houseplants in all other zones.

*Soil:* To make 2 quarts of soil medium, enough to pot 1 bulb in a 6-inch pot, mix together ⅔ quart peat moss, ⅔ quart packaged potting soil, and ⅔ quart sharp sand or perlite. Add ½ teaspoon of ground limestone.

*Light:* Southern exposure—requires at least 4 hours of direct sun a day during growing season.

*Moisture:* Water sparingly in spring, slowly increasing moisture during late spring. Water freely in summer. When foliage dies down after bloom, reduce water. When new foliage begins to emerge in the spring, resume watering.

*Humidity:* Moderate. Increase humidity during heating season.

*Temperature:* Cool. Prefers 50° to 60° F at night and 68° to 70° F in the daytime during winter heating season.

*Fertilizing:* Feed monthly from spring to fall with any liquid houseplant fertilizer. Each year, early in the summer, hose away some of the surface planting medium, without exposing the roots, and replace with fresh planting medium.

*Time to plant:* Spring.

*Planting instructions:* Since plant prefers potbound growing conditions, select a container no more than 2 inches larger in diameter than the bulb. Plant one bulb in a 6-inch pot or 3 bulbs in a 12-inch pot. Place an inch of drainage material in the bottom of the container. (You can use broken flowerpot shards, pebbles, or the plastic "popcorn" used by mail-order companies to ship goods.) Fill the bottom few inches of the pot with planting medium. Set the bulb so bulb neck will be above soil line. Fill the rest of the pot with planting medium to within an inch of the top of the pot. Water thoroughly.

*Postbloom care:* Remove faded flower petals and cut off entire blossom when it has turned yellow. After stalk has yellowed, cut it off. Using a hose, and without disturbing the root system, remove some of the surface planting medium in the pot and replace it with fresh medium. Withhold fertilizer and keep planting medium just barely moist. Normal summer indoor or outdoor temperatures and average light are appropriate. When growth resumes in spring, recommence regular watering and fertilizing.

*Bloom time:* Summer.

*Length of bloom:* 1 to 2 weeks.

*Propagation:* After 3 or 4 years, when it is time to repot, unpot plant when foliage has dried, remove offsets that have formed, and repot. Offsets may flower after 3 years.

*Chapter Eight*

# FORCING BULBS

Each year, in late winter or early spring, long before these bulbs bloom outdoors, you've probably noticed pots of blooming tulips, daffodils, and other bulbs on display at garden centers, nurseries, and florist shops. If you've ever wondered how bulbs are "forced," it is quite easy. You can do it at home by following these instructions. Just think of the joy of having your house filled with cheerful blooming spring bulbs in February and March.

As a rule, the pot should be about twice as deep as the length of a bulb. In other words, a bulb that measures 2 inches from top to bottom should be potted in a 4-inch-deep pot. See page 121 for how to treat new and used pots before planting in them.

## *SOIL MIXTURE*

A good soil mixture to use is Redi-Earth or Terra-lite, available in garden centers or nurseries, or you can use any other soil mix recommended for starting seedlings. If you wish to make your own soil mix, combine one-third packaged potting soil, one-third sphagnum peat moss, and one-third horticultural or builder's

## *SELECTING CONTAINERS*

Although you can grow bulbs in just about any kind of container imaginable, the traditional "bulb pan" of clay or plastic is probably the best; the essential drainage holes are usually provided.

sand. Add one cup perlite or horticultural vermiculite to each quart of soil mix. Be sure to wet the sphagnum peat moss thoroughly and squeeze until almost dry before adding it to your homemade mix.

## PLANTING

First, cover the drainage holes in the bottoms of the pots with pebbles, rocks, broken flowerpot shards, or the white plastic "popcorn" used by mail-order houses to ship merchandise. Then fill the pot about two-thirds full with soil mix. Set a bulb so the tip of it is half an inch below the rim of the pot. Adjust the soil level if necessary. Set more bulbs on the soil; make sure they do not touch each other. Fill the pot with soil mix. Do not firm it; bulb roots require loosely packed soil to grow properly.

If you are planting tulip bulbs, it pays to take special care in placing the bulbs in the pot. The first leaves tulip bulbs produce grow from the flat side of the bulb, so place the bulbs with their flat sides facing the outside of the pot. The ultimate effect will be more aesthetically pleasing, with the large leaves serving as an outer display of foliage.

Once planted, the bulbs should be watered thoroughly. Fill in cavities with more soil mix if necessary. Be sure to label each pot, so when it comes time to force bloom you will know which is which.

## THE CHILLING PROCESS

In order to bring bulbs to bloom before their normal time, you must provide a cool environment. In nature, when bulbs are planted in the garden, they require below-freezing temperatures in order to bloom. There are three different ways to do this.

First, you can sink pots into a cold frame outdoors, covering with a six- to eight-inch layer of salt hay or sand. However, this entails making trips out to the garden in the dead of winter to check on progress. Often, in very cold weather, it is difficult to remove the protective covering because it is frozen stiff. However, if you have no other option, this is the way to do it.

Second, much easier and equally as effective is to place the pots in the cellar or in an unheated garage. The temperature ideally should stay between 30° and 50° F. Cover pots with newspaper so that no light falls on the bulbs. In general, the pots will need to be watered approximately every four weeks. Even so, it is a good idea to check the soil every week; if it is dry to the touch, water moderately. Good root growth is essential for successful forcing; when in doubt, favor the longer rooting periods recommended in the individual entries.

The third method is to chill in a refrigerator. Simply place the potted bulbs inside and check every now and then to see if watering is necessary. Do *not* place pots in the freezer.

## FORCING BLOOM

After the prescribed cooling period, when shoots have emerged and are about two to three inches in height, it is time to bring the pots into warmer temperatures to begin the forcing process. The shoots will be a light yellow-green color. Although each bulb is handled slightly differently, the general procedure is to place the pots in a cool location, either in darkness or in bright, indirect light, for a period of three to five weeks.

During this period, bulbs will develop strong top growth. Check soil occasionally and water if necessary. (Note: To assure tall stems on hyacinths, rather than short stubby ones, fashion a cylinder about eight inches tall by one and a half inches in diameter out of heavy paper and place it over the emerging hyacinth flower stem. The semidark condition will cause the stem to elongate, thus looking more natural. When the stem is about six inches high, remove the cylinder.)

As soon as flower buds appear, place the pots in a location with cool temperatures (50° to 65° F) and direct sunlight. Once the buds begin to show color, they can be moved wherever they will be admired. Keep in mind, though, the cooler the temperatures, especially at night, the longer the bulbs will stay in bloom. Under optimum conditions—no warmer than 65° F—plants should stay in bloom for a week to ten days.

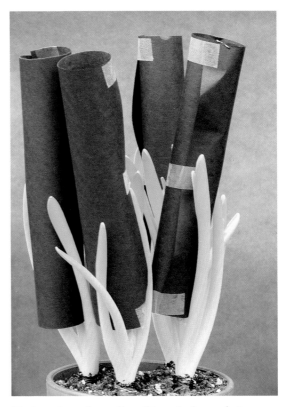

*To lengthen the stalks of hyacinths to their natural height, place black paper collars around the stalks after they have begun to grow.*

## POSTBLOOM CARE

Although tulips almost never bloom again once they have been forced—and should be discarded—other bulbs will bloom in your garden a year or two after forcing. However, they cannot be forced again the following year. And if you wish to plant the bulbs for outdoor enjoyment, you must care for them. After the flowers begin to fade, feed once with a liquid plant fertilizer according to the manufacturer's instructions. When the flowers are spent, cut the stems off at the soil line. *Do not* cut the foliage. Continue watering moderately until the foliage withers and turns brown. When the foliage is completely withered, remove the bulbs from the pot, cut off all the foliage and roots, and remove the soil. Place the bulbs in paper bags with labels, making a few holes in the bags for ventilation, and store in a dark, dry place until fall, when you can plant them in the ground.

## RECOMMENDED VARIETIES

Some varieties of bulbs are more suited to forcing than others. The Netherlands Flower Bulb Information Center recommends the following cultivars and the best-sized bulbs to use.

- Dutch crocus: Almost all cultivars can be used, but the following are recommended. Use nine-centimeter or larger bulbs.

  'Flower Record' (lavender)
  'Jeanne d'Arc' (white)
  'Large Yellow' (yellow)
  'Peter Pan' (white)
  'Pickwick' (striped)
  'Remembrance' (lavender)
  'Victor Hugo' (lavender)

- Hyacinths: Use bulbs that are $^{17}/_{18}$ and $^{18}/_{19}$ centimeter for earliest forcing and purchase bulbs that are prechilled. They are the easiest to force.

  'Amsterdam' (red)
  'Anna Marie' (pink)
  'Carnegie' (white)
  'Delft Blue' (blue)
  'L'Innocence' (white)
  'Ostara' (blue)
  'Pink Pearl' (pink)

- *Iris danfordiae* and *I. reticulata:* All cultivars are suitable, but 'Harmony' is perhaps best. Use six-centimeter or larger bulbs.
- *Muscari armeniacum:* Use nine- or ten-centimeter bulbs.
- Narcissus (large trumpets): Use DN I– or DN II–sized bulbs.

  'Dutch Master' (yellow)
  'Explorer' (yellow)
  'Golden Harvest' (yellow)
  'Mt. Hood' (white)
  'Unsurpassable' (yellow)

- Narcissus (large-cupped): Use DN I– or DN II–sized bulbs.

  'Carlton' (yellow)
  'Flower Record' (white with orange cup)
  'Ice Follies' (white)
  'Yellow Sun' (yellow)

- Narcissus (small cupped): Use DN I– or DN II–sized bulbs.

  'Barrett Browning' (white with orange cup)

- Narcissus (double): Use DN I– or DN II–sized bulbs.

  'Bridal Crown' (white perianth with orange center)

- Narcissus (miniatures): Use DN I– or DN II–sized bulbs.

  'February Gold' (yellow)
  'Jack Snipe' (white perianth with yellow trumpet)
  'Peeping Tom' (yellow)
  'Tête-à-Tête' (yellow)

- Tulips: Use bulbs that are twelve centimeters and larger.

  Red:
    'Bing Crosby'
    'Capri'
    'Cassini'
    'Charles'
    'Paul Richter'
    'Prominence'
    'Ruby Red'
    'Trance'
  Pink or rose:
    'Blenda'
    'Cantor'
    'Christmas Marvel'
    'Gander'
    'Preludium'
  Yellow:
    'Bellona'
    'Golden Melody'
    'Kareol'
    'Monte Carlo'
  White:
    'Hibernia'
    'Pax'
    'Snowstar'
  Lavender:
    'Atilla'
    'Prince Charles'
  Orange:
    'Orange Monarch'

*'Apricot Beauty,' perhaps the most popular tulip of all, not only provides color for the outdoor garden but can be forced successfully for indoor enjoyment during the mid- to late-winter season.*

Apricot:
  'Apricot Beauty'
Bicolored red and white:
  'Leen Van Der Mark'
  'Lucky Strike'
  'Merry Widow'
  'Mirjoran'
Bicolored red and yellow:
  'Abra'
  'Golden Mirjoran'
  'Kees Nelis'
  'Thule'

*Spanking white Dutch crocus 'Jeanne d'Arc' forces easily and can be used in combination with any of the more flamboyantly colored forced tulips or daffodils in an indoor display.*

# TIMING

If you want to have bulbs in bloom on a particular date, pay special attention to the last column on the accompanying chart. If, for example, you want to have hyacinths in bloom for a New Year's Day event, count back eight to thirteen weeks to arrive at a planting date—some time in the first two weeks of October would be safe. The cold rooting period offers some leeway, but never force bulbs that haven't been in the cold for the minimum number of weeks specified in the chart. You can, however, leave them in longer than the maximum number of weeks recommended, if necessary. If you order bulbs that have been prechilled, you can subtract approximately two weeks from the cold rooting period and one week from the time needed for forcing.

## Convallaria
LILY OF THE VALLEY

In order to force lilies of the valley, you must purchase pretreated bulbs from mail-order sources. Because the treatment the bulbs receive is complicated, you cannot readily do this yourself. Occasionally, local nurseries or garden centers also offer them. They are preplanted in containers. Simply follow the instructions included.

## Crocus (Dutch)

*Rooting:* 6 to 10 weeks in a dark location, at 30° to 50° F until shoots are 1½ inches tall.
*Forcing:* Bright, indirect light and 50° to 55° F temperature for approximately 1 week.

Move to full sun, cool (50° to 55° F) location until buds show color.
*Flowering:* Move to indirect light, cool temperatures (55° to 60° F) for longest flowering.
*Total weeks to flowering:* 9 to 13.

## Hyacinthus orientalis
DUTCH HYACINTH

*Rooting:* 6 to 10 weeks at 30° to 50° F in a dark location.
*Forcing:* 10 days to 2 weeks at 50° to 55° F in a dark location. Move into bright, indirect light when shoots are 4 to 5 inches tall. Buds should show color in 7 to 10 days. See page 135 on fashioning cylinders for elongating hyacinth stems.

A different method of forcing can be used for hyacinths: it involves a specially designed glass container filled with water. In midwinter, prechilled hyacinths are usually available at garden centers and nurseries; some mail-order sources also offer them. For best results, use only these bulbs.

Containers for them are also available at retail outlets. These are made of glass and shaped something like an egg cup. You set the bulb on a small upper section; the lower, larger section should be filled with water.

To start your hyacinths growing, fill the bottom of the hyacinth glass with just enough water to touch the base of the bulb. Place a piece of activated charcoal in the water to prevent the formation of algae. Place the glass in a cool, dark place, around 55° F until the root system is well developed and growth from the top has begun. Be sure to check the water level every few days and add more water to keep the level just beneath the base of the bulb.

When growth has commenced, move the

*This single forced hyacinth, 'Pink Pearl,' not only adds beauty to its surroundings but perfumes the air with its sweet, fresh scent.*

glasses to a room with lots of light and relatively cool temperatures, around 65° to 68° F. The hyacinths should bloom in 3 to 4 months. After bloom, discard the bulbs; they will not bloom again.

*Flowering:* Keep in bright, indirect light at 60° to 65° F for longest flowering.

*Total weeks to flowering:* 8 to 13.

## Muscari armeniacum
### GRAPE HYACINTH

*Rooting:* 6 to 10 weeks in a dark location, at 30° to 50° F, until shoots are 1½ inches tall.

*Forcing:* Bright, indirect light and temperature of 50° to 55° F for approximately 1 week. Move to full sun, cool (50° to 60° F) location until buds show color.

*Flowering:* Move to indirect light, cool temperatures (55° to 60° F) for longest flowering.

*Total weeks to flowering:* 10 to 14.

## Hardy Narcissus, Including Daffodils

*Rooting:* 10 to 12 weeks in dark location at 30° to 50° F. Shoots should be 3 to 4 inches tall before moving into light.

*Forcing:* Bright, indirect light and a temperature of 60° to 65° F for 3 or 4 days, then full sun until blossoms open, approximately 3 to 5 weeks.

*Flowering:* Move back into bright, indirect light at 55° to 70° F to prolong flowers.

*Total weeks to flowering:* 13 to 17.

## Narcissus tazetta
### PAPERWHITES

Paperwhite narcissus are among the easiest of bulbs to force. They are available all over the country in garden centers and nurseries in late fall and on into the winter. They are virtually foolproof and provide flowering plants for almost any kind of indoor environment. Some mail-order

Narcissus tazetta, *commonly called paperwhites, are easy to force and provide springlike bloom from early to late winter, depending on when you plant them.*

houses offer preplanted narcissus in bulb pans. All you have to do to bring them to bloom is to provide certain basic growing conditions. Unlike narcissus, daffodils, tulips, and other spring-blooming bulbs that can be forced, once paperwhites have bloomed, they will not bloom again, either indoors or planted in the garden, so dispose of them and purchase new ones the following year.

When bulbs arrive by mail or after purchasing, store in a cool, dark place until ready to plant. The refrigerator is good; do not, however, store them in the freezer.

*Rooting:* When ready to plant, select a shallow bulb pan or container *without drainage holes.* Tender narcissus grow well in pebbles, small stones, or broken flowerpot shards. Rinse all materials thoroughly until the draining water is clear. Place about an inch of planting material in the bottom of the bulb pan. Set the bulbs 1½ to 2 inches apart so ⅔ of the bulb is covered with material. Fill the bulb container about half full with water, allow to settle for about ½ hour, then pour off any excess by gently tipping the container. Place in a cool location, with little or no light and no risk of frost, for about 2 weeks. Test root development by gently turning the bulbs. Every few days check the moistness of the planting medium. If it feels dry to the touch, add a little water.

*Forcing:* When bulbs are firmly rooted, move pots to a location with strong light but no direct sunlight. Occasionally, the vigorous roots will actually heave the bulbs out of the planting medium. If this happens, gently work them down and add more planting material if necessary. Do not force them down or you will injure the tender roots.

*Flowering:* Once they are in bloom, they can be moved to any location, including one with little light.

*Total weeks to flowering:* 3 to 5 weeks, depending on variety and time of year. Those started from October to December take 4 to 5 weeks to flower. Those started from January to March take 3 to 4 weeks to flower; however, the stems will be shorter.

## Recommended Paperwhites

Some of the below have been so recently hybridized—those marked with an asterisk (*)—that they are not yet available at garden centers and nurseries or through mail-order sources. However, they should begin to appear in the marketplace within a year or two.

| CULTIVAR | COLOR | HEIGHT |
|---|---|---|
| 'Bethlehem' (also called 'Nony') | White with pale yellow center | 8–12″ |
| 'Galilee'* | White | 10–12″ |
| 'Grand Soleil d'Or' | Yellow and orange | 12–14″ |
| 'Israel' (also called 'Omri') | Creamy yellow with paler center | 14–16″ |
| 'Jerusalem'* | Pure white | 16–18″ |
| 'Nazareth'* | Cream and yellow | 10–14″ |
| 'Ziva' | White | 16″ |

## Tulips

*Rooting:* 12 to 14 weeks at approximately 30° to 50° F in a dark location.

*Forcing:* Approximately 10 days to 2 weeks in cool (55° to 60° F) location in bright, indirect light. Move to full sun, same temperature, for 2 weeks or until buds show color.

*Flowering:* Bright indirect light at 60° to 65° F for longest flowering.

*Total weeks to flowering:* 14 to 16.

# Bulbs Gathered in the Wild That May Be or May Become Endangered Species

Some of the wild-gathered bulbs listed below are also cultivated in Holland. Gardeners who do not wish to purchase bulbs harvested from the wild should avoid packages from Dutch growers marked "Bulbs from Wild Source." Those not so marked have been cultivated in Holland. In 1992, cultivated minor bulbs will bear labels of origin and will be marked "Bulbs Grown from Cultivated Stock" or "Bulbs from Wild Source." In 1995, major bulbs—tulips, daffodils, Dutch crocuses, and hyacinths—will also be marked "Bulbs Grown from Cultivated Stock."

Not all the bulbs listed below are sold by Dutch companies. Bulb sellers in other countries are not bound to the labeling agreement between the Dutch bulb industry and environmental groups in the United States and Great Britain, so the buyer must beware.

- *Anemone blanda*
- *Cyclamen*, except *Cyclamen persicum*
- *Eranthis cilicica*
- *E. hymenalis*
- *Galanthus*, except *Galanthus nivalis*
- *Leucojum aestivum*
- *L. vernum*
- *Narcissus asturiensis*
- *N. bulbocodium* var. *conspicuus*
- *N. b.* subspecies *tenuifolius*
- *N. cyclamineus*
- *N. juncifolius*
- *N. rupicola*
- *N. scaberulus*
- *N. triandrus* var. *albus*
- *N. t.* var. *concolor*
- *Sternbergia*

# Mail-Order Sources

## For Bulbs

Daffodil Mart, Brent & Becky Heath, Rt. 3, Box 794, Gloucester, VA 23061. Phone: (804) 693-3966

> For the daffodil enthusiast or hobbyist, a wide selection of hard-to-find daffodils is offered here.

John Scheepers, Inc., 63 Wall St., New York, NY 10005. Phone: (212) 422-1177/(212) 422-2299

> Lily-of-the-valley pips pretreated for forcing, calla lilies, gloriosa lilies, sprekelia, and other indoor bulbs are offered, along with an extensive selection of spring- and summer-blooming bulbs.

McClure & Zimmerman, 1422 West Thorndale, Chicago, IL 60660. Phone: (414) 326-4220

> Hard-to-find winter-blooming lachenalia is available here, along with many "minor" bulbs. Order early in the fall, as supplies are very limited.

Park Seed Co., Cokesbury Rd., Greenwood, SC 29647-0001. Phone: (800) 845-3366

> A large selection of spring- and summer-blooming bulbs with some winter-blooming as well.

Smith & Hawken, 25 Corte Madera, Mill Valley, CA 94941. Phone: (415) 383-2000.

> Only recently, this fine mail-order house has begun to offer bulbs. Some unusual types are offered.

Van Bourgondien Bros., Box A, 245 Farmingdale Rd., Rt. 109, Babylon, NY 11702. Phone: (800) 873-9444 outside New York; (800) 284-9333 in New York only.

> The largest selection of bulbs available in the United States and the prices are very reasonable. Hard-to-find winter-blooming clivia, freesia, and sprekelia are available here.

W. Atlee Burpee Co., 300 Park Ave., Warminster, PA 18974. Phone: (215) 674-4900.

This granddaddy of the mail-order seed and plant business offers a wide selection of spring-, summer-, and winter-blooming bulbs.

Wayside Gardens, 1 Garden Lane, Hodges, SC 29695-0001. Phone: (800) 845-1124

Hard-to-find winter-blooming crinum and valotta are available here.

White Flower Farm, Litchfield, CT 06759-0050. Phone: (800) 888-7756

Beyond their fine offerings of spring- and summer-blooming bulbs, this house offers hard-to-find winter-blooming clivia in pots, as well as agapanthus and freesia.

## For Perennials

Bluestone Perennials, 7211 Middle Ridge Road, Madison, OH 44057. Phone: (800) 852-5243

One of the best sources for perennial plants at very reasonable prices. These are small plants, available in either three-pack or six-pack. All plants are guaranteed to reach you in good condition and to grow. If they do not, the company will reship immediately or refund your money if you are not satisfied.

Klehm Nursery, Box 197, Penny Road, Route 5, South Barrington, IL, 60010-9555. Phone: (800) 553-3715

A specialty house, offering exceptionally beautiful and hard-to-find varieties of peonies, tree peonies, daylilies, iris, hosta, ornamental grasses and perennials.

# Index